Quaker and Naturalist Too

Quaker and Naturalist Too

Os Cresson

Foreword by David Boulton

Morning Walk Press
Iowa City, Iowa

The author's income from sales of this book will be
donated to the Nontheist Friends Planning Group, or the
Nontheist Friends Network UK, or Quaker Earthcare Witness, or will
be used to publish and market additional copies of the book.

.

Published by Morning Walk Press
Iowa City, Iowa
oscresson@juno.com
ISBN: 978-0-9914344-0-4
Typeset by Sara T. Sauers

Cover: "Home and Gallery" by Sarah Dowell in
Monteverde, Costa Rica. For more than 20 years I lived
a short walk through the woods from the home
and gallery of my good friend, Sarah.

All that is harmony for thee, O Universe, is in harmony with me as well. Nothing that comes at the right time for thee is too early or too late for me. Everything is fruit to me that thy seasons bring, O Nature. All things come of thee, have their being in thee, and return to thee.

—Marcus Aurelius (p. 113, below)

Contents

Foreword

For more than twenty years Os Cresson has been a leading light among nontheist Friends, his quiet, unassuming influence extending to Friends' communities in the United States, Britain and beyond. Os is a one-hundred-per-cent Quaker, a member of the Religious Society of Friends—and a one-hundred-per-cent naturalist without a trace of supernaturalism or mystical transcendentalism in his make-up. Not half-Quaker and half-atheist, not in two minds, nor standing with feet planted in two opposing camps, but "a person whose philosophies of science and religion and everything else are bound to what we observe and what we infer from that."

Clear as he is about his own position [he quotes the Oxford English Dictionary definition of naturalism: "A view of the world, and of man's relation to it, in which only the operation of natural (as opposed to supernatural or spiritual) laws and forces is admitted or assumed"] he is equally clear that this is only one position among many to be found in the modern, liberal, creedless Society of Friends. Os delights in this diversity and would have it no other way. Dogmatism is religion's most relentless enemy within, and readers will find no trace of it in this book.

Os has never thrust himself into the limelight. He has written for *Friends Journal* and contributed two classic essays to *Godless for God's Sake: Nontheism in Contemporary Quakerism*, the book which might be said to have given nontheist Quakerism lift-off when it was published in 2006, but many of his most valuable and insightful contributions have appeared in the transient medium of the internet, on the email forum nontheist-friends@googlegroups.com and the website http://www.nontheistfriends.org. One reason for welcoming this book is that it snatches some of these gems from cyberspace and gives them new life on the printed page.

The result is not only a powerful personal exposition of religious commitment free of outdated supernaturalism but also something of a handbook for nontheist Friends of all descriptions—naturalist, humanist, atheist, devout skeptic—and an eye-opener for Friends who have found it hard to reconcile godlessness with traditional Quaker metaphysics. Os starts with a short section on Quaker unity, but I would recommend coming back to that after first taking in a truly wonderful essay, "Quakers from the Viewpoint of a Naturalist," which opens his second section. This is probably the best short statement of what it means to be a nontheist Friend that I have read anywhere.

In a third section, Os digs deep into Quaker history to reveal a developing strand of Quaker dissent, or open-mindedness, which he characterises as the roots which eventually flowered into Quaker nontheism. Here he builds on one of his *Godless for God's Sake* essays, starting with Gerrard Winstanley and Jacob Bauthumley in the 17th century, moving on to 18th century "Quaker Skeptics" like John Bartram, the "proto-Hicksites" Job Scott, Abraham Shackleton, Hannah Barnard and Mary Newhall, and the Free Quakers of Philadelphia. In the 19th century he rediscovers David Duncan and the Manchester Free Friends, the Progressive and Congregational Friends of Longwood and New York, and the redoubtable Lucretia Mott ("I confess to great scepticism as to any account or story, which conflicts with the unvarying natural laws of God in his creation.") Among several 20th century radicals he includes Henry Joel Cadbury, historian, Biblical scholar, social activist ("I can describe myself as no ardent theist or atheist. . . . My own religion is mainly neither emotional nor rational but expresses itself habitually, or occasionally in action.") This section concludes with an essay on religious naturalism in the time of Fox. Os does not claim these giants for fully-developed naturalism or humanism, but offers them as examples of a free-thinking movement at the heart of the Quaker tradition which paved the way to an inclusive Quakerism where today's nontheist Friends can find themselves at home. Here he has made a most valuable contribution to Quaker historiography, the more so since each entry is backed by source notes including an extensive bibliography.

No less valuable is the list of more than fifty recent books, pamphlets, articles and essays by Quaker nontheists which brings the book to a close. This combination of exposition and resource manual makes *Quaker and Naturalist Too* a must-read both for Friends already committed to a nontheist viewpoint and others willing to explore adventurously what it might mean to be both religious and godless, Quaker and atheist. I cannot recommend it too highly.

—David Boulton

David Boulton is a member of Brigflatts local meeting in England, the author or editor of 22 books including The Trouble with God, Who on Earth was Jesus? *and* Godless for God's Sake: Nonthiesm in Contemporary Quakerism. *He is Convenor of the Nontheist Friends Network (UK) and 2012–13 President of Friends Historical Society (UK).*

Preface

I write in support of people who call themselves naturalists and seek a religious home within the Religious Society of Friends. This is also written to support all who seek harmony in Friends communities.

Ever since childhood, a few years after my birth in 1941, I have loved nature and loved being among Quakers. Nature fascinated me and I wondered how it worked. When this was described in school, I extended the explanation to everything, including us. Studies followed with degrees in biology (Earlham College, 1964), human learning (The Experimental College of the Institute for Behavioral Research, 1979), and applied behavior analysis, also called behavioral psychology (Western Michigan University, 1994). I worked as a teacher with people who had special educational needs, and am now retired and living in Iowa City, Iowa.

During all this time I was a Quaker. Our family attended meeting in our home and the homes of friends until I was 15 when we joined Radnor Monthly Meeting in Pennsylvania. After leaving my parents' home I stopped attending meeting regularly because my naturalistic explanation of what was going on was so different from that of other Quakers and I was not prepared to work on this with Friends who disagreed. Then my parents and I moved to Monteverde, Costa Rica, where we lived for 23 years. In the embrace of that community I became involved with Friends again. Slowly I began to talk with others about nature and Quakers. It was a big help to read a reprint in *Friends Journal* of Jesse Holmes's 1928 appeal for Friends outreach to scientists.*

---

*Jesse H. Holmes, "To the Scientifically-Minded," *Friends Journal* 38, no. 6 (June 1992): 22–23, http://www.friendsjournal.org.

I began to wonder about the Quakers who had been on nature walks like mine in the past, and who might be there now.

This was followed by a sojourn at Pendle Hill Quaker Study Center in 1995, "Nontheism Among Friends" workshops at the Friends General Conference annual Gatherings, conferences at Pendle Hill and at Woodbrooke Quaker Study Centre, and work with nontheist Friends on a website and email discussion group. Then, in 2005 and 2006, twenty-seven of us joined in writing a book.[*]

I found that nontheist Friends are as diverse a group as theist Friends. We enjoy being among the many varieties of Friends and do not seek to remake the Religious Society of Friends in our image. Like other Friends, we seek to learn about practices that can build unity in diverse communities. I was surprised that so few nontheists extending their skepticism about the supernatural from religion into psychology. They seemed to know little about science as it applies to human behavior.

This led me to write letters and articles and, eventually, this book. The essays here are grouped under the headings of unity, Quakers and naturalists, and history. Unity refers to unity Quakers seek in meeting for worship for attention to business, as well as unity in a loving and diverse community. The section on Quakers and naturalists is about my efforts to find a single harmonious philosophy that supports the life of a Quaker naturalist, and to share this with others. In the final section are a review of the writings of nontheist Friends and their forerunners, and a collection of excerpts from the writings of religious naturalists in the time of Fox.

This book is for those who love nature and Quakers, and for their friends who may not agree with them but seek to love and support them.

—Os Cresson
Iowa City, Iowa
February 9, 2014

---

[*]David Boulton, ed., *Godless for God's Sake: Nontheism in Contemporary Quakerism* (Dent, Cumbria, UK: Dale Historical Monographs, 2006).

Unity

The silence of the Quaker meeting for worship can be an experience of unity. I am an orthodox, garden variety Christian; I find the image of God first in Jesus the Christ. But it is my joy in the silent meeting to seek with those who find different ways to express the inexpressible truths of religious experience. Words can divide us, but the silence can bring us together. Whatever kinds of community the world needs, it surely needs the kind that embraces human diversity.—Parker J. Palmer (p. 18)

A note about
Sharing Meeting

Soon after starting to speak publicly as a nontheist Friend I asked to join Monteverde Monthly Meeting in Costa Rica where I had been a sojourning member for many years. I wrote to the members describing my nontheism and asked them about it during meeting for worship for attention to business when my membership was being considered. The clerk's reply was, "Os, it is you we love!"

Later, after moving from Monteverde to Mount Holly, New Jersey, I asked the local meeting to consider my becoming a member. A clearness committee was formed and I did some writing and shared it with them. One member of the clearness committee became upset and published a letter in Friends Journal *in August 2000 urging Friends to keep atheists and secular humanists out of our Society. I considered various replies but finally simply stated what was foremost in my heart at that moment. My letter,* Sharing Meeting, *was published in* Friends Journal *in January 2001 (47, no. 1, p. 5).*

During this time I encountered an essay by Henry Cadbury that led me to appreciate him and to study his writings.* In difficult situations I try to follow his lead.

Many Friends in Mount Holly were a great help including John Kriebel, Ed Dreby, Margaret Mansfield, Miriam and David Schwartz, Karen and Bill Robbins, Chris Darlington, Toby Riley and Sue Thorpe.

---

*Henry J. Cadbury, "My Personal Religion," *Universalist Friend* 35 (Fall-Winter 2000): 22—31, corrections in 36 (Spring-Summer 2000): 18. Also see Os Cresson, "Henry Joel Cadbury: No Assurance of God or Immortality," in *Godless for God's Sake: Nontheism in Contemporary Quakerism*, ed. David Boulton (Dent, Cumbria, UK: Dale Historical Monographs, 2006), 85-90.

Sharing Meeting

People of different religious beliefs can love each other. This has been shown many times.

I am particularly moved when sharing meeting for worship with people of a variety of faiths. One person's life may be centered on people, another's on an abstract principle, another's on a supreme being—but we are all present, waiting, loving each other.

I treasure the diversity among Friends and our unity in loving one another.

Osborn Cresson
Mount Holly, N.J.

A note about
On Quaker Unity

When I was eight years old I stared through a bus window at men down on their knees in the dirt facing the setting sun. This was in Afghanistan where my parents were teachers. I asked Mother what they were doing and she said, "They are doing what we do in meeting." After that our family settled into silent worship whenever the bus stopped for prayers.

Bridging differences has been important to me ever since, especially in Monteverde where I had intimate friendships with Catholics and Pentecostals and "none of the aboves," as well as many varieties of Quakers.

By early 2009, I had moved to Iowa City and was getting to know Friends in the meeting there and in West Branch, Iowa. I noticed some Friends biting their tongues so as not to offend me, which was unnecessary and perhaps damaging. This led to my writing a long paper that was boiled down to essentials and became "On Quaker Unity," published in Friends Journal *in July 2009.**

---

*Os Cresson, "On Quaker Unity," *Friends Journal* 55, no. 7 (July 2009): 5.

On Quaker Unity

Unity during meeting for worship for attention to business is familiar to Quakers. It is a commitment to move forward together and, significantly, it does not mean we have to hold the same views. This method of doing business has long been characteristic of Quakers.

To my surprise, the approach also applies to another kind of unity—that of the meeting community. The two senses of the word are fundamentally one: unity during meeting for business is the formation of a small community around a particular issue; unity of the meeting community is a commitment to each other and to our lives together.

There are many implications of applying what we know of unity in meeting for business to the life of the meeting community. One is that we do not need to agree. We can differ—in fact, we need to know when we differ and acknowledge it. Unity based on silence about our differences is not unity.

At first it struck me as remarkable that the concerted action of a faith community does not require agreement on faith, but we all know people who disagree and still love each other and act together. We see this in families that embrace different faiths. We also see it when we worship with those with whom we disagree—something we do every week. And this is not new: looking back through history we see people manifesting excellent values accompanied by different faiths.

There have been many varieties of Quakers and there still are, even within individual meetings. Differences in religious experience do not prevent cooperation. Shared practice does not require a shared explanation of the practice; we just have to love each other as we love those who believe as we do. Common purposes do not require a common religious language; we can each speak and write as we are moved, responding to the essence of what we hear and read rather than to its specific form.

Lives can stand in for beliefs. To find our collective identity as Quakers we can look to our shared lives. Membership does not have to signify that we hold the same beliefs but it can simply be an acknowledgement of the place of the meeting in the life of the individual, and of the individual in the life of the meeting.

All this seems paradoxical because we have thought of unity of belief as the path to unity of action, but Quakers know that unity does not require unanimity. Quaker unity is larger than that.

The embrace of religious diversity in our midst can be our gift to the world around us where differences in belief matter so much. Let us be patterns of living together and loving each other, differences and all. Let us openly and joyfully celebrate our peculiar combination of Quaker diversity and Quaker unity.

A note about
Listening and Speaking from the Heart

*In 2010 I joined Quaker Earthcare Witness, the environmental orga-
nization. There I found many varieties of Friends including some who
were critical of science as the cause of today's problems. Friends in
QEW did not seem to be embracing their differences. The Spiritual
Nurturance Committee worked on this, gradually coming to understand each other better. It was a heartfelt moment I will always remember when, after two years work, we approved our* Statement on
Unity with Diversity. *It is in the May-June 2013 issue of* BeFriending
Creation, *online at the QEW website, http://www.quakerearthcare
.org (see p. 102, below).*

*During this time I wrote about Friends practices that support uni-
ty. This became "Listening and Speaking from the Heart," published
in* Friends Journal *in 2013.* A few afterthoughts have been added in
the version here.*

*I don't know when I first heard or thought the phrase "listening
and speaking from the heart." It could have been from a member of
the QEW Spiritual Nurturance Committee, who might have seen it
in the pamphlet,* Practicing the Art of Compassionate Listening.**

*I am grateful for the loving support of the members of the com-
mittee as well as many others, including Roy Treadway, Richard
Grossman, Louis Cox, and Callie Marsh.*

---

*Os Cresson, "Listening and Speaking from the Heart," *Friends Journal* 59,
no. 5. (May 2013): 5.
**Andrea S. Cohen, Leah Green, and Susan Partnow, *Practicing the Art
of Compassionate Listening* (Indianola, WA: The Compassionate Listening
Project, 2011).

Listening and Speaking from the Heart

In relations among Friends I encourage us all to practice listening from the heart and speaking from the heart. By this I mean hearing someone speak their accustomed words, and transposing into your own terms as you listen, and then replying as you are led while the other person listens.

This also applies to reading and writing. It involves individual words, and phrases, and messages as a whole.

In this relationship we each speak freely, as we do during meeting for worship. We respond to the source and purpose of words rather than their particular form, to the spirit rather than the letter. We support Friends whose beliefs differ from our own as strongly as we support Friends whose beliefs we share.

In Costa Rica before a trip my friends sometimes bless me in the name of various Catholic saints. I deeply appreciate their desire to do all they can to keep me safe. Although the entities and powers they invoke are imaginary from my point of view, I sincerely thank them and wish them well in my own naturalistic terms.

This contrasts with our usual practice of ignoring or hiding differences, limiting dialogue to terms we all agree on. Keeping the peace by keeping quiet is the norm in society at large and in some Quaker meetings and organizations, and it may be necessary in an emergency, but it can be a false peace. There is a better way.

Listening and speaking from the heart is built on experiences we all have had. We all know people living good lives accompanied by a great variety of beliefs. We know that today and through history many varieties of Friends have lived as Quakers. We see people loving across differences. We reach the same point by different paths, and we cooperate even as we speak differently about what we are doing. We worship with Friends with whom we disagree. Experiences like these sustain our search for innovative ways to embrace unity amid diversity.

As speakers speak and listeners translate, the burden of not offending each other shifts from the speaker toward the listener. It can shift back when listeners haven't learned about our way of speaking and listening, or are too distraught to remember. With visitors and the very young, and when writing for the general public, we need to avoid speaking and writing from a particular framework of belief unless we have made it clear that this is but one of many viewpoints in our diverse group. When we speak for the group, we speak from a larger heart than just our own.

When we write statements for possible approval by a diverse group, we can include religious sentiments about which our members differ but we must clearly label them as such. These sections can be preceded and followed by phrases that inform the reader that these are views some of our members hold. The test is whether uninformed readers interpret from the heart.

In a loving community, unity does not require agreement on our various approaches to life. It can be simply a matter of moving forward together. We are familiar with unity in this sense in our meetings for worship for attention to business. Our shared practices and purposes bind us together as a group. Our identity as Friends is evident in the life of our community, rather than in our words. Membership in our community is a sign of our commitment to each other.

Listening and speaking and reading and writing from the heart can be a great help in many situations. It can facilitate intrafaith dialogue in Friends meetings and organizations and families. It applies to differences in religion and philosophy and politics and values. You may ask, What does God require of me?, while I ask, What is required of me? You can work for change by organizing the 99%, and I work by quietly building friendships with particular individuals. You may be a Pentecostal pastor and I an atheist Friend and yet we join in loving a person living with HIV/AIDS. Starting from the heart doesn't resolve our differences, but it helps us work together, which can be a significant step forward.

Elements of this practice are well known to Quakers, as in our emphasis on listening, and on speaking as led. This is how we worship. It is in the ways we love our neighbors. We try to care about both the needs of the individual and the needs of the community of individuals. We are skeptical of words that divide, turning instead to simple friendship.

Let us unite in faith based action even as our faiths differ. Let the many kinds of Friends worship together, and practice collective discernment, and in other ways be Friends together. Let our rich variety of experiences be a blessing for our group. Let us openly and joyfully celebrate our unity amid diversity.

A note about
Listening and Speaking from the Heart:
An Anthology

I enjoy reading one topic in the writings of many authors, in a sense reading horizontally rather than vertically. Sometimes this leads to new insight. On other occasions, when the author is struggling with problems I am facing, this encourages me and I resolve to keep on working.

It is important to remember, the excerpts shown here are taken out of context and may not reflect the full views of the authors.

Friends, may these words lift you as they have lifted me.

Listening and Speaking from the Heart: An Anthology

Listening, speaking, reading, and writing from the heart are ways Friends interact in diverse families, meetings, and organizations. This can take place during worship and in conversations. It is a way to be individuals and a community at the same time.

In this practice we each speak in our own characteristic way, and as we listen we interpret in our own terms. Our replies are guided by where words we hear are coming from and going to, and by the main point of the message rather than the accompanying beliefs.

Elements of this approach are in many Quaker writings. Here are examples arranged in four groups: (a) listening from the heart, (b) speaking from the heart, (c) variety of language and belief among Friends, and (d) unity based on practices and testimonies.

Listening from the heart

On the evening of the 18th I was at their meeting, where pure gospel love was felt, to the tendering of some of our hearts. The interpreters endeavored to acquaint the people with what I said, in short sentences, but found some difficulty, as none of them were quite perfect in the English and Delaware tongues, so they helped one another, and we labored along, Divine love attending. Afterwards, feeling my mind covered with the spirit of prayer, I told the interpreters that I found it in my heart to pray to God, and believed, if I prayed aright, he would hear me; and I expressed my willingness for them to omit interpreting; so our meeting ended with a degree of Divine love. Before the people went out, I observed Papunehang . . .

speaking to one of the interpreters, and I was afterwards told that he said in substance as follows: "I love to feel where words come from."

—John Woolman[1]

Holy listening—to "listen" another's soul into life, into a condition of disclosure and discovery, may be almost the greatest service that any human being ever performs for another.

—Douglas Steere[2]

Listening creates a holy silence. When you listen generously to people, they can hear truth in themselves, often for the first time. And in the silence of listening, you can know yourself in everyone. Eventually, you may be able to hear, in everyone and beyond everyone, the unseen singing softly to itself and to you.

—Rachel Naomi Remen[3]

The second chapter of Acts tells the familiar story of Pentecost, when the Holy Spirit descended upon the early church in the form of a roaring wind and "tongues of fire". What happened next is often referred to as "speaking in tongues": the apostles were able to preach the gospel in such a way that everyone understood their words, even if they did not speak the same language. But implied in the story is that those who heard were able to "listen in tongues", able to hear and understand, even though the language spoken was unknown to them. Pentecostals consider speaking in tongues to be a *charism*, a gift of the Spirit. Perhaps we Quakers have been given the *charism* of "listening in tongues." Sometimes what we interpret as conflict is really just a longing to be heard, to be acknowledged, to be understood, to be listened to. If we can respond to that longing, then sometimes the hard edge of our differences can be considerably softened.

—Tom Gates[4]

We must listen and listen and listen. We must listen for the Truth in our opponent, and we must acknowledge it. After we have listened long enough, openly enough, and with the desire to really hear, we may be given the opportunity to speak our truth. We may even have the opportunity to be heard. For no one and no one side is the sole repository of Truth. But each of us has a spark of it within.

—Gene Knudsen Hoffman[5]

Quakers join other mystical traditions in knowing that spiritual union happens more through listening than talking, more through experiencing than formulating, more through surrender than control.

—George Lakey[6]

Speaking from the heart

[W]e wait, in silence of the fleshly part, to hear with the new ear what God shall please to speak inwardly in our own hearts, or outwardly through others, who speak with the new tongue which he unlooseth and teacheth to speak; and we pray in the spirit, and with a new understanding, as God pleaseth to quicken, draw forth, and open our hearts towards himself.

—Isaac Penington[7]

We [Congregational Friends] allow the utmost liberty of speech. . . . We do not TOLERATE but INVITE and ENCOURAGE the free expression of thought and opinion. We love this freedom and rejoice therein as our most precious jewel. And why should not those who differ from each other in doctrine come together, not to wrangle and dispute, but to compare views in the spirit of love, and aid one another in the search for truth?

—Oliver Johnson[8]

There is a way of life so hid with Christ in God that in the midst of the day's business one is inwardly lifting brief prayers, short ejaculations of praise, subdued whispers of adoration and of tender love to the Beyond that is within. No one need know about it. I only speak to you because it is a sacred trust, not mine but to be given to others. One can live in a well-nigh continuous state of unworded prayer, directed toward God, directed toward people and enterprises we have on our heart. . . . Now out from this holy Center come the commissions of life. Our fellowship with God issues in world-concern. We cannot keep the love of God to ourselves. It spills over. It quickens us. It makes us see the world's needs anew. We love people and we grieve to see them blind when they might be seeing, asleep with all the world's comforts when they ought to be awake and living sacrificially, accepting the world's good as their right when they really hold them only in temporary trust. It is because from this holy Center we relove people, relove our neighbors as ourselves, that we are bestirred to be means of their awakening.

—Thomas R. Kelly[9]

We seek to access and convey our own deep truth from as close to our own heart as we can get. The language we choose reflects a healing intention rather than words of blame or judgment that may trigger another's defenses. If we seek more information, it is out of genuine curiosity rather than to disprove the other person's point of view. We reframe issues to get at the essence of underlying needs and feelings. We courageously choose to give voice to what has truth and meaning—and do all of this for the sake of promoting healing.

—Andrea S. Cohen, Leah Green, and Susan Partnow [10]

Do not take offence because others disagree with you. Be chary of ascribing, even in your mind, unworthy motives to others. Try not to take things personally. Promote the spirit of friendship in the meeting so that Friends may speak their minds freely, confident that they will not be misinterpreted or misunderstood.

> —*The Yearly Meeting of the Religious Society of Friends (Quakers) in Britain*[11]

Variety of language and belief among Friends

And oh, how sweet and pleasant it is to the truly spiritual eye to see several sorts of believers, several forms of Christians in the school of Christ, every one learning their own lesson, performing their own peculiar service, and knowing, owning, and loving one another in their several places and different performances to their Master . . . For this is the true ground of love and unity, not that such a man walks and does just as I do, but because I feel the same Spirit and Life in him, and that he walks in his rank, in his own order, in his proper way and place of subjection to that; and this is far more pleasing to me than if he walked just in that track wherein I walk.

> —*Isaac Penington*[12]

We cannot make the world more beautiful by trying to paint it all of one hue; we must learn to see that variety is the characteristic of a universe of endless originality of form. Instead of being pained and shocked, it is better to listen patiently and say our own wisest thoughts as well as we can.

> —*Joseph B. Forster*[13]

Quakers do not share a fixed set of beliefs. Our unity is based on shared understanding and a shared practice of worship, not on our beliefs all being the same. There is no need to be in unity with Quakers on every issue in order to be part of our meetings. There is a great diversity within the Quakers on conceptions of God, and we use different kinds of language to describe religious experience. Some Quakers have a conception of God which is similar to that of orthodox Christians, and would use similar language. Others are happy to use God-centred language, but would conceive of God in very different terms to the traditional Christian trinity. Some describe themselves as agnostics, or humanists, or non-theists and describe their experiences in ways that avoid the use of the word God entirely. Quaker faith is built on experience and Quakers would generally hold that it is the spiritual experience which is central to Quaker worship, and not the use of a particular form of words (whether that be "God" or anything else).

—*The Yearly Meeting of the Religious Society
of Friends (Quakers) in Britain* [14]

Are you comfortable with a Society whose unity of spirit coexists with a diversity of beliefs? Are you prepared to join a Meeting family which includes people whose perspectives may differ considerably from yours?

—*Philadelphia Yearly Meeting*[15]

The silence of the Quaker meeting for worship can be an experience of unity. I am an orthodox, garden variety Christian; I find the image of God first in Jesus the Christ. But it is my joy in the silent meeting to seek with those who find different ways to express the inexpressible truths of religious experience. Words can divide us, but the silence can bring us together. Whatever kinds of community the world needs, it surely needs the kind that embraces human diversity.

—*Parker J. Palmer*[16]

In the original sense of the word we should be evangelists, carriers of the good news. And what is the "good news"? Is it not that we are brothers and sisters, with an equality of status in our search for a good way of life, and that none of us can claim to have "the only true faith" which others must accept in order to enter into that fellowship of life and hope? It seems to me that the term "quietism" would be more appropriate to those who would withdraw or remain withdrawn in limited associations of belief while the world is anxiously searching for the grounds of unity. Should Quakers receive the Good Samaritan into membership? Yes, if his or her life is consistent with the action in the parable. And in many cases the life is consistent, whether it be the life of Samaritan, Moslem, Buddhist, Confucian or "pagan" animist in Africa.

—Arthur Morgan[17]

[S]lowly, and agonizingly, over the past three hundred years we have had to learn how to live with uncertainty: with the realisation that we may be mistaken and that, though there may be contingent truths and untruths, there is no absolute, unchanging truth, no Truth with a capital T. Truth, we have learnt, is itself diverse, and is to be made rather than found. Whatever seems to speak to our condition, to ring true, that is our truth for the time being, and will remain so until our condition changes, until new bells ring out new truths. We have a theology that no one view is absolutely "right", even the view we most cherish. Truth is relative and cultural. Of course it is. We now wonder how it could ever have been thought to be anything else.

—David Boulton[18]

A particular strength of Quakerism has been its ability to adapt to changing times without losing the insights which it has gained from the past. One of the striking changes that has taken place over the last century is that there is now vastly more opportunity for people with different backgrounds to meet and exchange ideas; and, this being so, it would be sad if those brought up in Jewish, Buddhist, Moslem or other traditions—and indeed those with no religious upbringing of any kind—were excluded at the outset from full participation in the affairs of the Society. I would suggest that further thought be given to ways of ensuring that such people are positively welcomed into the Society. No one is being asked to give up any cherished conviction: those who wish to retain traditional Christian beliefs are in no way being discouraged from doing so; and, indeed, for many people this may be the right and only road to travel. I hope, however, that such people will be willing to worship alongside those who—if they break the silence at all—might choose to use somewhat different forms of language. One could perhaps say that, in an important sense, universalism comes "not to destroy . . . but to fulfil." [Matthew 5:17]

—*Tim Miles*[19]

I suppose that to be completely honest, the amount of Christianity that you have, and the amount of Quakerism, in the last resort is your own selection out of those two orbits of what has come to appeal to you. Nobody can put down in writing either for a Christian or a Quaker what he has to be. He can put down in writing some of the things he can honestly attribute to those two groups; and we select from them, unconsciously I'm sure, those features which are congenial to us. I guess you know that in the Society of Friends people select very different things.

—*Henry J. Cadbury*[20]

(P)resent-day Quakerism owes a special debt to those interpreters who do justice to more than one of its multiple strands, the mystical, the evangelical, the rational and the social. . . . It would be a pity if the natural variety in Quakerism were artificially restrained. Even unconsciously we are subject to powerful tendencies to conform to a single standard in religion as well as in other ideologies and practices. If the role of Quakerism among the denominations is precisely one of enriching the variety and challenging their standards of uniformity, we ought by the same token to welcome variety within our own small body and ought to object to the impoverishing effect of attempting to get ourselves and our fellow Quakers into one mould.

—*Henry J. Cadbury*[21]

Perhaps it is given to us to show how a great people can be gathered into a unified and loving community while respecting, and even celebrating, its individual members' distinctiveness. But one thing is certain—we Friends cannot preach reconciliation in the world at large unless we ourselves are reconciled.

—*Daniel A. Seeger*[22]

The Multwood Group helped me frame some queries for ourselves as we expand and reach outward, and for any others who would seek to enter into a similar experiment: *Are we willing to approach one another without expectations, waiting on the Holy Spirit as long as necessary? Are we willing to accept the limitless and surprising ways God can work in the world? Are we willing to speak with integrity from our own experience and honor the authenticity of another's experience? Are we willing to be present to one another despite the discomfort of differing beliefs, language, or culture, and continue to be open as long as it takes for the group to find its own center in God? Are we willing to listen with an open heart and be vulnerable to being changed as well as to the potential of changing others?*

—*Margery Post Abbott*[23]

Unity based on practices and testimonies

In the Religious Society of Friends we commit ourselves not to words but to a way.

—*The Yearly Meeting of the Religious Society of Friends (Quakers) in Britain*[24]

We do not have a creed. . . . Rather, we are held together by the way in which we are a religious group, what I have called a "behavioral creed": the way we worship and do business and areas of testimony.

—*Ben Pink Dandelion*[25]

21

The history of all religions indicates that religion is more what it does than what it thinks. People who differ in their thinking can worship together in harmony, if the manner of worship is congenial to all. At the time of Christ, for example, a Jew might be an atheist; he might be a Platonist; he might have one of many types of religious philosophy. But as a Jew his membership was defined by his practices rather than by his opinions. This seems to be true in most religions. . . . Religion is more a matter of experience and practice than of thought. Religion begins in experience; systematic thought comes later. . . . So there is no need for us to feel baffled by the variety of opinions among us.

—*Howard Brinton*[26]

(T)he best way of advertising any ideal is to wrap it up in a person, to incarnate it. Vocal or verbal Quakerism cannot compete with incarnate Quakerism.

—*Henry J. Cadbury*[27]

I want to make a proposal. It will not provide us with all we need to say, but it will, I think, give us a starting point and it will point us in the right direction. My proposal is that we recover the meaning of our distinctive practices. If we have largely lost a distinctive way of speaking, we at least still have a distinctive set of practices. We still meet together in silence, we listen to one another without criticism, we wait for discernment in important decisions we make, we seek a common mind when we have decisions to make together, we act against violence without using violence ourselves, we refuse to give in to cynicism when we seek to make changes in the world. And we accept responsibility for one another. These are all disciplines, or rather, aspects of one discipline for the conduct of our lives. And as a discipline these practices indicate more clearly than anything else what distinguishes Quakers from other religious groups, and they suggest, though not very clearly, what Quakers are positively committed to. Our first task, I want to suggest, is to find a way of saying what those practices mean. This at least gives us a focus and a basis in experience for saying what we have to say. But it is not just a practical convenience to focus on our practice. It is clear from our history that Quakers have chosen to express their faith mainly in a way of life. Their spirituality has always been a practical discipline, one that can be lived in the everyday world. So we can be thankful that this practical discipline has survived, at least in its formal structure. This no doubt is what in practice holds our meetings and Society together. It is also—whether we recognize it or not—what gives us our identity. But of course, without an account of what the discipline means, it can only be a vague and confused identity.

—*Rex Ambler*[28]

What I am saying is this: The search for doctrinal unity, for Truth with a capital T, is pointless because it will be fruitless. If earlier Quaker generations cobbled together a one Truth they could witness to, it was a Truth which could be maintained only by discipline, and which changed subtly from generation to generation. Quakers today are, or should be, free from the tyranny of that kind of Truth: true doctrine. The spirit leads us in different directions, because our faith is experiential, and our experiences, backgrounds, temperaments, capacities differ widely. The spirit which leads us into all truths—there are a lot of them, and they never stay the same—has itself become diverse, experimental, exploratory, for we have begun to understand that this spirit is not some independent entity, external to ourselves, but one that lives and moves and has its being in the infinite diversity of our human consciousness. Does this mean, then that there can never be any basis whatever for any kind of Quaker unity? Surely not. It simply means that we do not need doctrinal unity or faith in a doctrinal Truth. Our unity, our group or subculture identity, depends on something different. I believe that the "something different" is the shared sense of belonging to a particular tradition, focused on the manner in which Quakers choose to meet for worship, meditation or contemplation—call it what we will. Quakers in Britain are people who choose to meet in this particular unprogrammed way, people whose current needs, preferences, temperaments lead them to get something out of, and hopefully put something into, this particular (and rather arcane) ritual. That, and nothing more (but nothing less), is the basis of our unity. That is our bottom line.

—*David Boulton*[29]

Given this history of divisiveness, I can see why Friends are wary about identifying themselves as Christian or non-Christian. It seems safer, and saner, to keep Christ and God talk to a minimum. I am glad that many Friends are willing to bring up these concerns, however. I think we can be better Quakers if we are honest and admit our differences and have respectful dialogues about theological issues. We can learn much from each other when we open up and share our beliefs and spiritual experiences. And I think we can communicate with those in the ecumenical and interfaith movement, as well as our neighbors of other faiths, when we feel comfortable talking about theology among ourselves in a Friendly, non-exclusive way.... If Friends cannot unite around theology, could we instead unite around practices like peacemaking and social justice? George Fox said we need to be "salt" and "light"...To be "salt and light," we need to transcend our differences. We need to share our stories, listen to those we disagree with, and be open to a change of heart. We also need to seek common ground wherein we can put our faith into practice.

— *Anthony Manousos*[30]

I'm sure the meaning of being a nontheist among Friends is different from nation to nation, from community to community, from person to person, but for me it starts with individual relationships, one on one. If being an openly Nontheist Friend was just about bringing in a set of ideas in hopes of influencing a religion, however true and important I might think those ideas are, I would have lost interest in the subject years ago.

Rather, it is about revealing our true selves to one another, and listening as others reveal their true selves to us. I think this revealing is the most genuine purpose of community, of religion. The fact that our true selves are different in important ways, and that those differences sometimes lead to disagreement and conflict, is a strength in our community, not a weakness. If we all believed the same things, what could we possibly learn from each other?

The love in our communities, if we are lucky enough to have it, is not theological or theoretical. It is not philosophical or right or wrong. It is real, human, messy, and conflicted. If we focus solely on our commonalities, our areas of agreement, there is only so deep we can go. I would like us to go deeper. I think we can handle it.

—*James Riemermann*[31]

Quakers and Naturalists

We feel the need to seek from within a loving and traditionally tolerant, gathered community.

—Workshop for Non-Theistic Friends (p. 93)

A note about
Quakers from the Viewpoint of a Naturalist

For me, a naturalist is a person whose philosophies of science and religion and everything else are bound to what we observe and what we infer from that. Science is observation and the study of what we observe. Naturalism is the philosophy of science.

All labels have drawbacks. A naturalist can also be a person who studies biology in the wild, or who enjoys nudity. I don't mind being mistaken for either of them, but I try to make clear that I am referring to a person who seeks a naturalistic explanation of our human condition.

Quakers from the Viewpoint of a Naturalist *was in a set of essays I wrote during the clearness process when applying for membership in Mount Holly Monthly Meeting and as preparation for a nontheist workshop at the 2000 Friends General Conference Gathering. The essays were submitted to* Friends Journal *but they decided not to use them. Five years later their editor called and asked if I could combine two of the pieces for an issue they were doing on the variety of belief among Friends. The ones he wanted were the story of my journey as a Quaker naturalist, and my description of the essentials of Quakerism from a naturalist's perspective. I added a draft minute on unity and diversity that I hoped Friends meetings and organizations would consider. This appeared in* Friends Journal *in 2006.**

Robert Dockhorn, Daniel A. Seeger and Katherine Rush were especially helpful as I wrote this.

---

*Os Cresson, "Quakers from the Viewpoint of a Naturalist," *Friends Journal* 52, no. 3 (March 2006): 18-20.

Quakers from the Viewpoint of a Naturalist

I grew up loving nature and feeling part of it—dirt, bugs, people, and everything. It was, and still is, amazing how the universe simply rolls along, no miracles required. You and I are orderly, physical events, like the weather.

People have always fascinated me. How surprising to see the cousins of apes doing all this! Unfortunately, a naturalistic approach to human behavior left me with a big problem: how to motivate myself when meaning isn't simply handed to me. The issue wasn't the existence of God, but of free will. This took ten years to work out. Finally, I saw that it is enough to live meaningfully, behaving as do those who find meaning in other realms. I care just as much as they do and share many of their values and purposes even as I accept that my behavior is the universe dancing with itself, and nothing else.

I also grew up loving Quakers. About once a week we held a meeting for worship that we children called "quiet time." It was in our home or that of neighbors because we lived far from a meetinghouse. Ours was a religion of daily life and I was allowed, even expected, to hold my own views. I was skeptical of the Quaker tradition of reaching beyond the physical to the spiritual and supernatural. This seemed unnecessary, but it was the way others find comfort in a difficult world—it was more of the marvelous diversity around us.

I noticed that Quaker behavior is available to all who would engage in it. This includes those who view it not as based in the supernatural, but as the behavior of an animal that has learned to wait in the silence and to follow leadings and so on. It is still wonderful and worthy of study and imitation.

As I have lived among Friends, certain characteristic Quaker behaviors have become apparent. I look at Quakers from the viewpoint of a naturalist. I see them in terms of observed behavior and the environments in which it occurs, rather than resorting to concepts from other levels beyond sense and reason.

We are passionate in our determination that each and every person merits our tender concern and that in each person is an element of goodness to which we can appeal. We search for what is essential in our lives, and we treasure what each other find. There is no need for special training to do this.

These commitments affect all aspects of our lives. We wish to live lovingly and to love effectively. We witness to new possibilities in peace and education and human rights, to healthy communities and respect for the rest of nature, to simplicity and honesty and justice. We hope that our lives will speak of what we believe.

We accept people searching for truth and are not dissuaded by differences in the words with which we express the truths we find. We bind ourselves to no creed. Membership is a question of participation in the meeting community rather than how we talk about our faith. We are a diverse community.

Quaker faith is newly created in each of us. The results of our searches are colored by the conditions under which we search, the people involved, and the times. We commit to one another and we hold together as change goes on around and within us.

Collectively we worship, we celebrate in joy and sorrow, and we carry forward the business of the meeting. While worshiping, we try to yield our personal agendas. In the shared silence we wait to respond. The silence leads to messages and common purposes and action in the wider world.

We encourage learning and seek understanding of how nature, including humankind, works and how to mend it when there are problems. We seek to find appropriate ethical standards and to help each other hold to them.

We try to simplify our lives. This includes how we worship and think and relate to people and the rest of the environment.

This, then, is what I have seen Quakers doing. It is usually described in mystical terms, but some Quakers try to stick with what is obvious. Suns rise, birds sing, and Quakers worship. It is so simple.

For many years I was quiet about all this among Friends, not wanting to create a scene and doubting there were others who shared this approach. Even Quaker environmentalists seemed to be spiritualizing nature rather than naturalizing religion. This was one reason I held back from very much involvement in my Quaker meeting. Living as a Quaker was enough.

Then, in June 1992, as I walked into my parents' home, Mother thrust a copy of *Friends Journal* into my hands, saying, "You'll want to read that!" It was a reprint of Jesse Holmes's 1928 appeal to scientists who might be interested in Quakers. He wrote, "It is a Society of *Friends*. Friends claim no authority but owe each other friendliness. . . . Our unity consists, therefore, in having a common purpose, not a common creed . . . God is . . . the name of certain common experiences of mankind by which they are bound together into unity."

Suddenly I realized there had been naturalistic Quakers in the past and there probably were many of them today. The issue keeping me from Friends became a reason to reach out to them. I shivered at the thought.

This led to a sojourn at Pendle Hill and a search for those who love nature above all else, and who love being Quaker too. It turned out there are many and they are welcome in many meetings. I began to speak up and was sharply criticized a few times, and I began to feel empathy for Friends who are marginalized and to wonder how I could help.

Humankind today is being asked to consider a demotion, one in a series that have taken place during recent centuries. The question facing us is whether religion has to involve the supernatural. For me the experience of being part of the natural world is a religious experience. Atheists and other skeptics can lead good lives, good Quaker lives, and they can function well in our meeting communities. Quaker practices are available to us all, however we speak of them.

Sadly, naturalists who are not Quakers probably don't know they would be welcome in many meetings. Wouldn't it be a joy to declare this to the world?! Of course, we wouldn't want to limit it to one perspective. We could announce our commitment to diversity of all kinds including religious faith and experience. Many sorts of minutes might accomplish this; one is offered below.

A minute like this would be an invitation to all who wonder whether their religious experiences are acceptable among Friends. It would say: come and let us worship together and get to know each other. Let us try being Quaker together.

Let Each of Us Unite

To Friends Everywhere,

We, the members and attenders of this monthly meeting, gathered in a meeting for worship for attention to business on this day, unite in support of the following statements about membership in our meeting:

Decisions regarding membership are made by members and attenders participating in a clearness process. This includes the person or persons asking for membership. We seek to discern what is involved and what is appropriate for all concerned.

During this process we ask whether the applicant and the meeting are functioning well as a community. We look at how we live together as a monthly meeting and not at whether we have had the same religious experiences and hold the same beliefs.

We consider membership without being limited by the race, ethnicity, gender, sexual orientation, age, physical condition, education, economic status, criminal record, political views, or religious beliefs and experiences of the applicant. We are committed to love that overcomes differences. Diversity in our meeting is a wonderful thing.

As a diverse community we speak in different ways. We expect speakers to speak and listeners to translate. We hope that members and attenders of our meeting will not bite their tongues, but will express themselves freely in their several religious languages.

When speaking with visitors, or writing materials for them, we try to make clear that each person is responsible for listening carefully to, and interpreting for themselves, the religious expressions of others. Writings published or distributed by our meeting are meant to serve as guides rather than rules. We are all called on to express our religious views in our words and lives.

We describe the origins of this commitment to diversity in many ways. Some of us are led to it by the experience of the Divine in every person. Some are led by a conviction that all people are worthy. Some hold that the views expressed here are sufficient unto themselves and need no justification in other terms. All these approaches can work well for the people saying them and can address the same needs.*

Amid diversity we seek and find unity. We join in a sense of the meeting even as we differ. We join in action inspired by our different faiths. We commit ourselves to love one another and to live together in harmony.

It is with joy in our hearts that we declare this to the world.

---

*This paragraph is an example of a useful way to write for a diverse group. Individual views are bracketed by expressions of a desire to be inclusive. Other examples are in the excerpt on variety of belief in Britain Yearly Meeting, p. 17, above, and the "Statement on Unity with Diversity," *BeFriending Creation* (May-June 2013): 9, http://www.quakerearthcare.org.

A note about
Nature, as I See It

I have tried writing a unified theory of science and behavior many times. Each result seemed better than the last, but then I would find serious flaws. The topic and I have had a loving but difficult relationship.

Nature, as I See It *started as a long treatise and then was shortened a bit. That seemed to help, so I kept paring away. I like minimalism in painting and music, and in religion and science. It became my goal to simplify this statement as much as possible, while remaining at least minimally intelligible.*

Nature, as I See It

This is about my experience of nature, you, me, and everything else.

Our story begins with behavior (B) and environment (E).

E is all there is, or all we need. E is what we sense
and otherwise respond to. E is known to us when it evokes B.
E synonyms are matter/energy, nature, universe, and cosmos.
E encompasses humans as well as all the rest.
It is not just background.

B is bodily movement, other than being blown over in the wind, etc.
B is known to us when it causes changes in E.
B and E are defined in terms of each other:
B by E it controls, E by B it controls.

B and E are one, becoming two as we speak of them.
B is E happening. We are BEing.

E is always moving. Nothing is still.
E is ongoing, interlocking chains that feed back on themselves.

Scientists look for events caused by other events.
This is a deterministic approach, one that has worked well.
Determinism is a characteristic of the method,
not a statement about the universe.

Scientists explain E in E's own terms.
These are bound by the methods and data of science.
Our concepts are defined in terms of the operations that produce
them. We talk about observations, methods for making them,
conclusions about them, and nothing else.

This is a black-box approach.
We correlate B and the resulting changes in box E,
but we don't look inside the box.
When links in a causal chain are related,
we work with them even though we don't see the intervening links.
We don't speculate about realms beyond possible observation.

B is an event like other events, nothing more.
If the universe returned to the state it was in
when you started reading this line,
you would respond again as you have just responded.

Sensing is behaving, as is measuring and observing.
Also perceiving and experiencing.
Private events, like thinking and feeling,
are B sensed only by the BEing person.
B is a function of E on both sides of the skin.

E control of B can change when new combinations of E are introduced.
This is learning. There are many ways it happens.
Look where it has gotten us!

BEing is interlinked:
your B is part of my E and my B part of your E.

E today includes future E as we think about what may come.
B's E shapes future E.

My self is my BEing. No one is in charge.
The evidence for self is the set of facts self was invented to explain.
An autonomous self feels right, of course:
I hold my hand this way or that.
Most people wish they were in charge, trying to
aggrandize the human condition.

Mind, will, and consciousness are to psychology, what God is to religion.
Those who eschew speculation in one philosophy,
are wise to do so in all philosophies.

The behavior of looking ahead, weighing consequences
and trying hard is available to everyone,
including those who see themselves as E rolling along and nothing else.
We are each responsible for the consequences of our actions.
Meaning in our lives is seen in the lives we live.
Environmental explanations are supplanting imaginary ones.

E replaces a designing intelligence for the origin of life,
and the origin of species, and the origin of B.
Questions of heredity and environment become:
what E was involved in what ways.

Regarding what is not observed, we look for evidence
and for tools that help us look.
We assume what is unseen is more of the world seen,
until there is reason to assume otherwise.
We honor experiences of the supernatural,
even as we explain them as BEing.
The unseen will be known by its effects,
or it will remain unknown.

Science looks for natural causes
and avoids assertions about the supernatural.
As long as there have been records of human thought,
there have been contests between naturalists who accept
orderly events around and within us, and supernaturalists who call for
something else above and beyond us.
Since childhood I have been in the first group, happily.

For some of us, this is enough.
Nature is fascinating and inspiring.
In nature I seek a healthy, caring, productive, and pleasant life.
Feeling the unity of nature lifts me. When the sun rises, my heart sings.
This is central to my life as a naturalist and a Quaker.

For some of us, a purely environmental approach is not enough.
Those who feel this way can be naturalists in particular situations.

Nature, and the way of knowing nature that is science,
are available to all of us.

Our story started with E and B and BEing and went on from there.
I encourage us all to build E in which we learn more about nature.
Whether this happens and how it happens is up to us,
up to E shaping us and shaped by us.

A note about
Science Is . . .

Science Is . . . *is here to help you make sense of* Nature, as I See It.*

It is a pleasure to acknowledge the contribution of my science teachers, including Don Kingsbury, Clayton Farraday, William Stephenson, Cameron Gifford, Hugo Moser, Murray Sidman, Harold Cohen, Jack Michael, Galen Alessi, and Kay Campbell. I benefited indirectly from my mentors' mentors, Buckminster Fuller and B. F. Skinner.

Many science books gave powerful nudges along the way, includ-ing Mabel Pyne's The Little History of the Wide World, *Ralph and Mildred Buchsbaum's* Animals Without Backbones, *Moon, Mann and Otto's* Modern Biology, *Jacob Bronowski's* The Ascent of Man, *Alan Watt's* Joyous Cosmology, *and Theodore Benfey's* Friends and the World of Nature.

I give thanks to all.

---

* For another description of my position, see: Os Cresson, "Quaker in a Material World," Quaker Theology 5(1), Spring-Summer 2003, 23-54, http://quest.quaker.org.

Science Is . . .

Naturalism, as the philosophy of science, requires a clear statement of what science is.

In this essay I address the characteristics of science, its relation to values and religion, objections to science, and relations of scientists and nonscientists.

Characteristics of science

Science, as I have experienced it, is defined by three features: observations, causal relations, and behavior.

Observations. Science concerns itself with observations, and how we obtain them, and what we say about them, and nothing else.[32]

Ernst Mach, physicist and philosopher and forerunner of general relativity and logical positivism, wrote in 1883, "Faithful adherence to the method that led the greatest investigators of nature . . . to their great results, restricts physics to the expression of *actual facts*, and forbids the construction of hypotheses behind the facts, where nothing tangible and verifiable is found."[33] Bertrand Russell went further and wrote, "A habit of basing convictions upon evidence, and of giving to them only that degree of certainty which the evidence warrants, would, if it became general, cure most of the ills from which the world is suffering."[34]

Observations are produced by environmental events. Environment, also called nature, universe, and cosmos, is all we know. It gives rise to life, and it forms species over eons, and shapes behavior over lifetimes.

Scientists do not speculate about what is not observed. For instance, we take no stand on the supernatural. This was central to a court case on teaching Intelligent Design as an alternative to evolution in public school science classes. Quaker philosopher and biologist Robert T. Pennock testified that scientific method explains observable events in terms of natural causes without assuming the existence or nonexistence of the supernatural. He called this methodological naturalism. In the final decree, the judge, John E. Jones III, stated that since this is a ground rule of science, Intelligent Design is a form of theology rather than science.[35]

Scientists analyze what is observed because this is effective. Since science is limited to what is observed, the results are available for verification and integration into other fields. Speculation can't be tested, and can distract us from the environment in which we must act.

This is a black box approach. I became intimately acquainted with a black box fifty years ago and have never forgotten what it taught me about science. In freshman Chemistry at Earlham College we were given black boxes of different sizes and shapes. We were told to try every test we could think of and then describe a theoretical model that would function like our box. We were not to open the box, or to speculate about what was inside. We shook the boxes different ways and listened to sounds and felt vibrations. One student used a large magnetic field and another submerged a box in water. After a week of experimenting with the boxes and writing reports, our teacher offered to open one of them. After all, sometimes tools are invented that let us look into closed boxes. He reached in and pulled out . . . a smaller black box, smiled, and rattled it. I loved this approach, so simple and clear and safe. It seemed wise to behave this way until there is reason not to.

It works out well to respond to the unseen world in boxes as more of the seen world outside them. This is the world in which we were formed and it is where we live.

Scientists do not ignore what is not observed. We respond to what is offered as evidence of the unseen. We may extend the range of observations by looking in new places and in new ways. Experiments are carried out to demonstrate relations among observations. Sometimes we speculate in the sense of forming hypotheses to be tested, but this is bound to the world in which the test takes place. When we have to act in the absence of data, we interpret the unknown in terms of the known. There is still plenty of mystery in science, which is part of its attraction. Whether this is inherently unknowable cannot be answered.

Sometimes the best response in the presence of the unknown is to remain silent. As B. F. Skinner wrote, "Scientists have . . . discovered the value of remaining without an answer until a satisfactory one can be found. This is a difficult lesson. It takes considerable training to avoid premature conclusions, to refrain from making statements on insufficient evidence, and to avoid explanations which are pure invention."[36] We would be wise to take to heart the last line in Ludwig Wittgenstein's treatise on philosophy: "What we cannot speak about we must pass over in silence."[37]

Causal Relations. Environment is always changing. We have probably all been surprised to feel the gentle swaying of a tree we are leaning against. The entire forest is in motion.

One afternoon at Earlham College I was learning to use a Mettler balance, the most delicate weighing device we had. The lab manual instructed me to weigh an object three times. I used a glass beaker half-full of water. My results didn't agree with each other: the numbers kept getting smaller. Peering at the last wheel showing the smallest change in weight, I saw it was turning slowly. The scale was detecting molecules rising from the surface of the water. I gasped and looked around the room at the busy students and their equipment and the walls of the building: it was all moving!

Science is concerned with events turning into other events. Scientists seek to demonstrate causal relations and to make general statements about these relations that are useful in new contexts.

Claims are put to the test of experience. Honesty in reporting is critical. Others repeat and verify what has been found. This allows us to behave effectively and to predict what may happen and to participate in shaping our futures.

Of course, correlation is not necessarily causation. Birds sing early in the morning and traffic increases, but birds don't cause the traffic to increase. To demonstrate a functional relation we present an environmental event and see what environment results. The test is whether we can predict and control events. If so, we have demonstrated a functional relation as well as a correlation.

Events occur in ongoing chains in which each link is simultaneously an effect and a cause. These chains connect in networks made of links that can have multiple causes and multiple effects.

A wise psychologist wrote, "[W]e are not justified in assigning to anyone or anything the role of prime mover. Although it is necessary that science confine itself to selected segments in a continuous series of events, it is to the whole series that any interpretation must eventually apply." (This was B. F. Skinner in 1953.[38]) A wise Buddhist responded, "We are now listening to a man who represents himself as a behavioristically oriented, non-mystical, on-the-whole materialistic, hard-headed scientist. Yet this passage is the purest mysticism, which might have come straight from Mahayana Buddhism . . . No segment, no particular pattern of integrated behavior within whatever universe we are discussing can be called the prime mover. Now this is the Dharmadhatu doctrine of Mahayana Buddhism, that the universe is a harmonious system which has no governor, that it is an integrated organism but nobody is in charge of it. Its corollary is that everyone and everything is the prime mover." (This was Alan Watts in 1963.[39])

Behavior. The third defining feature of science as I know it is the inclusion of behavior in the realm of science. There is no good reason to set behavior apart from other events. Doing that leads to all sorts of speculation about its causes.

44

Behavior is bodily movement (aside from events in which the matter/energy of the immediate cause corresponds to that of the immediate effect, as when someone else lifts your arm). Behavior is an environmental event, a ripple in environment caused by other environmental events. We are waves in the continuum of Behavior and Environment. We are BEing.

We speak of behavior and environment as separate but that is only for convenience. The separation is in the eye (and behavior) of the beholder. As it says in the *Tao Te Ching*, "Naming is the origin of all particular things."[40] (All environmental control of behavior has this effect, not just naming.)

Behavior and environment are reciprocally related: environment shapes behavior, and behavior shapes environment. This happens between people when my behavior becomes part of your environment, and your behavior part of my environment. We set conditions in which desired behavior is likely, our own as well as that of others.

For a naturalist, environment includes humans. Environment is not just forests and mountains and sky; it is not just background. That way of talking is left over from the ancient effort to convince ourselves that we are distinct from and better than the rest of the world. Naturalists offer an inclusive language and an inclusive philosophy.

This topic is central to the story of human civilization. During the last 120 or so human generations, science has gradually moved through mathematics, astronomy, physics, medicine, chemistry, meteorology, geology, and biology, to finally arrive at behavior. Environmental explanations have replaced speculative ones for motions of the planets, changes in the surface of the earth, causes of disease, and the origins of life and of species. It is time to look to the environment for the origin of behavior. As everything we know involves human behavior, this will affect our entire culture. It will be a revolution to rival the industrial revolution.

Now that we are characterizing behavior as an environmental event, we can revisit our definition of science. Observing is behaving, like sensing, measuring, and experiencing. Science, as the behavior of scientists, is a human social enterprise. An early expression of this approach was by Percy Bridgman in 1927: "In general, we mean by any concept nothing more than a set of operations; the concept is synonymous with a corresponding set of operations."[41]

For naturalists, there is no self. No one is home. There is no I writing these words, or reading them. Writing and reading happen like everything else. There is no autonomous agent, no free will. We don't do anything. Doing simply happens. We have a poem as a mother has a child.[42]

If behavior is a natural event caused by other natural events, we can depend on it. As you read these lines we both expect certain sounds to be associated with certain letters. We repeat environments in which desirable things happened, hoping they will happen again.

As well as behaving, we learn to behave. Combinations of environment change the way environment controls behavior. Here are examples: we salivate in the presence of lemon juice, and when we think about lemons in the presence of the juice, thinking itself can come to elicit salivation. When behavior produces an improved environment, that behavior tends to be repeated. A word paired with rewards comes to function as a reward. These are some of the many combinations of behavior and environment that result in behavioral control passing from one environment to another.

A naturalist translates the traditional terms in which we talk of behavior. Language is BEing: the meaning of a word is found in the environments in which the word appears, in the function of the word. The meaning of a life is found in what we work for, our goals, values, and purposes. Statements are true when they help us behave effectively. For instance, our test of whether something is a true copy is how well we behave with the copy. Knowledge is effective behavior. Consciousness is what we say exists when we respond to our own behavior. To paraphrase René Descartes, "I think about my behavior, therefore I am."

46

Thinking and feeling are behavior, too, even though only sensed by the BEing organism. Other behavioral events are not observed by the person behaving and these we call subconscious. Behavior is a function of environment, whichever side of the skin it is on.[43]

When observed links in causal chains are related, we can work with them without observing the intervening links. In science, as in religion, our guidelines apply to inner as well as outer behavior. Jesus said, "Now do ye Pharisees make clean the outside of the cup and the platter; but your inward part is full of ravening and wickedness. Ye fools, did not he that made that which is without make that which is within also?"[44]

Science and values

For a scientist, values are what we work for. We hold to standards because the contingencies of our lives hold us there. Different scientists have different values. These are not inherent in science; they come with the people practicing the science.

I have noticed that Quaker environmentalists differ dramatically. There are those who favor immediate environmental action and those who want more discussion of underlying principles. Some work for reform and some for revolution. We work through personal contacts with insiders or by pressuring from the outside, and we may do so quietly or loudly.

These approaches are compatible when we acknowledge that we can come to the same point in very different ways, and we can cooperate as Friends and as environmentalists even as we speak differently about what we are doing.

I am sometimes asked if I believe in something bigger than myself. This probably doesn't mean bigger in size or power, but perhaps more important, or beyond my understanding. Yes, environment is all that for me. (I would replace "believe in" with "accept" or "behave as if there exists".)

The observed world provides a practical basis for values. Such values can be held just as consistently and stubbornly as values that are theoretical in origin.

The question arises, why try hard to live well in an inherently meaningless world? Not having an answer distressed me during my twenties. The world was clearly a wonderful place and I was thrilled to be part of it, but why strive as others are striving without the reasons they give for doing so? Finally, I saw that the behavior of those who think they are free to choose their actions is available to me too. Looking ahead, and weighing consequences, and trying hard are possible even though I am simply environment rolling along. I am affected by and responsible for the consequences of my actions. I generate meaning and purpose as I live.

For many Quakers and many scientists, theology and morality are not prescribed. They are worked out, lovingly, in each particular situation. This puts a great responsibility on each of us and on our communities as we seek truthful environments and truthful lives.

Science and religion

Religion is human behavior. Our behavior is accompanied by a wide variety of views. Even as we differ, we worship together, and comfort each other, and celebrate joys and sorrows, and unite in common purposes, and otherwise function as a religious community.*

Religion is often said to involve spirituality. Any word can be defined naturalistically, but whether or not I do so depends on how my listeners react. "Spiritual" can refer to what is essential to us, our highest principles, the heart of our world views. However, I do not speak of spirituality in this sense because for many of my listeners the word signifies something beyond the physical. This is not sur-

---

*This topic is developed further in my chapter, "Chanticleer's Call: Religion as a Naturalist Views It," in *Godless for God's Sake: Nontheism in Contemporary Quakerism*, David Boulton, ed. (Dent, Cumbria, UK: Dale Historical Monographs, 2006), pp. 37–42.

prising since that is why it was invented. In the *Oxford English Dictionary,* "naturalism," "naturalist," and "physical" are defined in contrast to "spiritual." (See Glossary on p. 131, below.) Also, for many of my listeners, "spiritual" is associated with "Spirit," a synonym for God, which brings further complications.

In both religion and science people have inspiring and reassuring experiences of unity with the universe. These moments are important to scientist and nonscientist alike. A sense of the unity of nature has provided a center of gravity holding my personal universe together, helping me live effectively and meaningfully. Time and again, a sunrise has lifted my spirits, as has the surprise of a boy who saw he could check his subtraction by adding up the results, and a woman who saw her reading problem vanish as she came to understand phonics. Ah, nature!

For some of us, nature is enough. My religion is wrapped in the same philosophy as my science. Thus, nontheism becomes a special case of the more general avoidance of speculation. Mind, will, and consciousness, except as metaphors for natural events, are private gods that I do without.

This would be a disappointment for some people. As Henry Cadbury noted, "To call the set of a man's life his religion no doubt seems a great comedown—when you are used to finding it in beliefs or distinctively religious experience. But when a man deals religiously with issues that others settle in other ways, in fact takes seriously the religious implications of behavior both individual and collective, tries to practice fully the standards that conventional religion officially endorses, and to make his whole life consistent if not conscious, he is in my opinion practicing religion as much as the one who skillfully builds the dialectic structure of a well rounded theology or as the man who through public and private devotion lives in that mystical drama of the religious imagination."[45]

A major religious innovation of the twenty-first century will be the growing acceptance of religion that doesn't involve the supernatural, and I hope the Religious Society of Friends will participate fully.

Objections to science

I am concerned for those among us who have strong reservations about science and what it represents in our world today. Some look for evidence in science itself to support their call for a reformation of the philosophy of science. This has been called ecospirituality, Deep Ecology, and the New Story.[46] These Friends are passionate environmentalists most of whose goals I heartily endorse.

An example is in the writing of Doris Ferm who was led to the following insights: we are all relatives; everything is in motion; life is amazing; God is in every creature; and this can lead us to love and protect nature. We need a new story that inspires us in novel ways and leads to a planetary culture based on our primary allegiance to the web of life.[47]

Friends, all these insights can be and have been achieved by people holding a variety of views, such as that God gave us nature to use for our own benefit, or that there is no God, and so on.

Here are a few comments on ways in which science is said to fail. Uncertainty at the quantum level is given as a reason to suppose human behavior can be freely willed. However, we don't know if the uncertainty is an artifact of our observational methods, or if something else is going on, and any link of quantum phenomena to the origin of human behavior is conjecture.

Science is criticized as objectifying nature but, since observing is behavior, there is no observing without subjective experience. The issue of subjective vs. objective becomes a matter of what is controlling the observing behavior.

It is suggested that the whole is greater than the sum of its parts. It is true that a car is greater than the sum of its parts since there are things you can only do with a car after it is assembled. When I teach you A=B and B=C, and you pair A and C with no additional instruction, this can be called an emergent phenomenon but it is still a natural event.[48]

Science is criticized as reductionistic, but I don't see why it is a problem to explain the biology of psychology, the chemistry of biology, the physics of chemistry, and so on. In any case, scientific fields can be independent of each other, with scientists in each field explaining their observations in their own terms. Another objection is that the interconnectedness of events in the universe makes accurate prediction impossible, but it is an empirical question whether the flutter of a butterfly in Costa Rica affects the observations I am making in Iowa. It is said that the close fit of organisms and the world they live in is too remarkable to be the product of the universe rolling along (the Anthropic Principle), but it would only be notable if these didn't fit since this is the world in which the organisms evolved.

Happily, we don't have to agree on philosophy to be Friends.

Quaker skepticism about science has been noted before. Kenneth Boulding, a scholar in residence at Pendle Hill in 1989, noted that although the "core culture" there was diverse and not oppressive, it involved "a certain hostility to science and a certain propensity for untested ideologies."[49]

The Religious Society of Friends, and Friends environmental organizations in particular, need us all. It would be good to apply what we have learned about the accommodation of our members' variety in theology to the accommodation of our variety in the philosophy of science.

Relations of scientists and nonscientists

Members of a Quaker family, meeting or organization may have different views on religion and science. The question is how to find unity in our diverse communities whatever the topics on which we differ. Practices that support unity can do so across many issues.

Looking back through history, Friends who helped create a Religious Society of Friends that accepts naturalists were usually not naturalists themselves. These forerunners supported views that eventually made it possible for me to be a Friend and a naturalist too. This included the views that Scripture has to be interpreted by the person reading them, that behaving like Christ is more important than notions about Christ, and that membership can be based on participation rather than doctrinal agreement.

Interestingly, whether specific views are natural or supernatural is a relative question. For example, a person might hold that souls are mortal, although these souls are not physical. A person might hold that God does not intervene in our lives, although God created the universe.

In our Society today, Friends of all kinds worship together. Our practices and testimonies are available to all. Our paths converge.

The path of science I am describing contrasts with the path suggested by Plato in his allegory of the cave. He described us as chained so we only see shadows formed on the back wall of the cave by objects moving in the sunlight behind our heads. For more than 2300 years people have followed Plato's lead. As Howard Brinton put it in *Quakers for 350 Years*, "The world of appearance and the world of reality . . . are different. Deceit arises when appearance takes the place of reality instead of being a genuine and sincere expression of it. . . . As Truth and Substance, [the Light] shines down from a world higher than our world of Deceit and Shadow, and guides us up toward itself."[50] In Brinton's writing, "reality" refers to the supernatural, and "appearance" refers to the ancient criticism that science is useful for predictions, "saving appearances," but does not explain the more important "reality."

Aristotle pointed out that Plato's explanation itself is unexplained, leaving us no better off. And we may be worse off if we are distracted from environments in which we have the problems and must find the solutions. Scientists, chained in caves like everyone else, try to invent ways to look over our shoulders, and when that doesn't work we behave as if what is back there is more of the world in front of us, the world of shadows, walls, slaves, and philosophers.

These two paths were exemplified by Rufus Jones and Henry

Cadbury. They shared a lot. Both were Quaker leaders in the early and mid-twentieth century. They helped found and guide the American Friends Service Committee and they worked for a generation to reunite divided Yearly Meetings. They were both associated with Haverford College for many years, and Rufus married Henry's sister, Elizabeth. However, they differed in their views on science and religion. Jones was passionate about direct experience of the Divine, and Cadbury was a closeted secular humanist.[51]

This is clear in their reactions to the phrase, "the imaginative dominion over experience". George Santayana wrote those words in describing the genius of poets and other artists, and they have been quoted often.[52] Here is what Rufus Jones wrote about the phrase, and about science and religion, in 1930:

> Those aspects of life and experience which we express in terms of personal intents and attitudes, of awe and wonder, of freedom and initiative, of joy and beauty, of love and grace, of inspiration and vision, of creative insight and flash of discovery, aspects by which we enlarge the entire range and scope of life, do not comfortably submit to the methods of science. We need poetry as well as fact. We need to achieve what has been called "imaginative dominion over experience," which produces greatness of life. None of us could live on the dry provender of analysis and description alone. A world that was only a "fact-world" with no visions of relief would drive us all into sheer insanity. That "imaginative dominion over experience" not only makes poets and prophets, but it keeps the race sane and normal, and enables us common mortals to walk the earth with a serene joy in love and beauty. Until someone shows how the scientific ladder, that is nothing but a scientific ladder, climbs up into the regions of unselfish love and beauty, we may well continue to insist that there are values of life which must be approached and appreciated by other ways of apprehension than those which are appropriate for discovering atoms and nebulae.[53]

Jones was so moved by the phrase "imaginative dominion over experience" that he quoted it in six other books.[54]

In 1936 Henry Cadbury commented on the phrase in notes for a talk, titled "My Personal Religion," that he prepared for his divinity students. He wrote,

> It seems to me that both theology and piety are interpretations. I recall the words of an American critic about poetry. Poetry, he says, is the imaginative dominion over experience. Perhaps religion is much the same—the dramatizing of life in terms of an unseen companion, or of a loving father, or of a greater creator. This dramatizating goes into all aspects of life. History, when religiously interpreted, means divine governance and intervention into affairs of men—particularly in the person of Jesus Christ. Strong natural sympathy for persons in need is interpreted in terms of intercessory prayer. Vivid conviction of duty is interpreted as a direct command of a personal god, and so forth.[55]

Cadbury never published this but his daughter, Elizabeth Musgrave, gave her permission for it to appear in *Universalist Friends* in 2000.

Eleven years after Jones died in 1948, Cadbury shared his views on Santayana's phrase with the public. He wrote,

> I think both [the evangelical and Inner Light] parties would feel less anxious about their difference if they could see the nature of religious expression and their several relations to it. "Poetry," wrote a literary critic, "is the imaginative dominion over experience." Much the same might be said of the language of religion. Whatever the experience—and all kinds of Friends like to feel the supremacy of experience—the expression of experience is an imaginative dramatization, in which supernatural beings and significant transactions are involved on a stage conceived as the dramatist does with the figures and actions of a play. Psychological phenomena

are described in terms of personification and action. These vivid descriptions are accepted as though they were realistic and objective events in space and time. Modern Biblical study has suggested the necessity of "demythologizing" much of the religious staging of those ancient records. It has not shown substantial reasons for ending just there instead of continuing the process in the modern world which retains so much of the same kind of imaginative construction.[56]

I feel gratitude to both these men for so clearly advocating their views. My approach contains some of Jones's mystical feeling, although in a naturalistic sense, and I try to continue Cadbury's demythologizing. Science, for me, is imaginative dominion by experience.

A note about
Quaker Outreach to Scientists

My work on Quaker Outreach to Scientists *started in 1992 when I read Jesse Holmes's 1928 essay, "To the Scientifically-Minded." Later I joined Quaker Earthcare Witness, the principle U. S. Quaker organization involved with science, and I was surprised. Many members wanted to reform science because they saw it as the cause of our environmental problems as well as our spiritual problems. We all loved nature, and we shared many goals, but they were spiritualizing nature while I was naturalizing religion.*

I felt a new urgency to speak to Quakers about science, and to scientists about Quakers.

Quaker Outreach to Scientists

I ask Friends to consider reaching out to scientists, encouraging them to seek a religious home among Friends. We seek people who will join in the life of our meetings and organizations. This doesn't mean we agree on the philosophy of religion or of science.

This outreach will be of particular interest to Friends in Quaker Earthcare Witness (QEW). As stated on their website, "Quaker Earthcare Witness is a network of Friends (Quakers) in North America and other like minded people who are taking spirit led action to address the ecological and social crises of the world from a spiritual perspective, emphasizing Quaker process and testimonies."[57] This is the most active U. S. national Quaker organization that directly addresses science issues. Quakerism can provide a religious home for scientists, and QEW can be the portal.

Here I address what Quakers and science offer each other, and some possible components of an outreach program to scientists.

What Quakers offer scientists

Quakers and scientists are seekers. They both emphasize direct unmediated experience. They try to be contemplative and inventive, and they are drawn to simple practices and explanations. They are bound into communities by shared practices and purposes.

Quakerism and science are both noncreedal. Quaker philosopher Elton Trueblood noted,

> It is a good part of the mood of science to seek to base conclusions upon experience rather than to make conclusions in advance of

experience or independent of it. It is this mood which makes the consistent scientist the enemy of all prejudice. Quakerism is the most striking application of this mood to religion.[58]

Quaker astronomer Jocelyn Bell Burnell has said,

> I find that Quakerism and research science fit together very, very well. In Quakerism you're expected to develop your own under-standing of God from your experience in the world. There isn't a creed, there isn't a dogma. There's an understanding but nothing as formal as a dogma or creed and this idea that you develop your own understanding also means that you keep redeveloping your understanding as you get more experience, and it seems to me that's very like what goes on in "the scientific method." You have a model of a star, it's an understanding, and you develop that model in the light of experiments and observations, and so in both you're expected to evolve your thinking. Nothing is static, nothing is final, everything is held provisionally.[59]

Both Quakers and scientists are passionately concerned about mending our world. They are fundamentally practical and often optimistic about the possibility of improvement. Friends offer an opportunity for social action by scientists, but this alone is not enough to attract scientists because there are many such opportunities open to scientists. Quakers will appeal to scientists who are drawn to Quaker practices and testimonies in general as well as to specific projects.

Scientists hold a variety of views about God, but there are more nontheists among them than in the population as a whole, and even more the further along they are in the study of science. A survey in 1996 showed 60.7% of scientists disbelieved or doubted God's existence. This rose to 93% among members of the National Academy of Sciences.[60] Thus, it is likely there are scientists who will appreciate hearing from Quaker meetings and organizations that welcome nontheists.

What scientists offer Quakers

To accomplish Friends environmental goals it will help to know more about environment, and how it works, and how people are studying it. Friends and scientists can unite in their love of environment and their desire to live well as part of it.

Science offers a narrative that starts with our place in nature. It is an environmental explanation of the human condition. Environment is the source of human action.

Quakers will benefit from the focus of science on events. As Kenneth Boulding wrote, "[W]e are undoubtedly hampered by the use of an Indo-Aryan language which is so riddled with the sub-ject-verb-object structure that we have to use an absurd expression like 'it is raining' when there is no 'it' at all, but simply an activity. If we could make God into a verb instead of a noun a great many linguistic obstacles to the practice of religion in the modern world might be removed."[61]

Science is concerned with observed events rather than entities, powers or concepts invented to explain them. In like manner, our Quaker practices are available for everyone, whatever explanatory theories they favor.

Science will be more important in the future because of issues such as climate change, access to resources, and technology in our lives. As the science of human behavior becomes better known, science will become more relevant in psychology and in religion. Science education is vital for our future.

As the Religious Society of Friends seeks to interpret its message for new generations, it will help to incorporate the narrative given us by science. This is particularly true in Friends environmental organizations and in our schools.*

---

* For more, see: Os Cresson, "Quakers and the Environment: Three Options" (unpublished manuscript, 2005), http://www.nontheistfriends.org.

An outreach program

I suggest that, in addition to our general outreach, we reach out to scientists specifically. There are many other groups that can also be the focus of targeted outreach, such as youth, Christian Friends and Latin American Friends.

Outreach starts with in-reach: what practices make it easier for us to be a diverse Quaker community? How diverse are we prepared to be? How do we respond to the questions a scientist might ask? How do we represent the entire Religious Society of Friends and yet speak honestly as individuals?

The Religious Society of Friends will be stronger if we welcome everyone who participates in our programs and activities, and if we make this clear to visitors. This means that, as a group, we do not endorse particular scientific or religious philosophies.

Methodological science avoids assertions about what is not observed. We can differ in our opinions about the universe and still cooperate in our practice as scientists. This opens a path to unity even as we differ in areas that are not science.

There is precedent for Quaker outreach to scientists. This was a concern of Jesse Herman Holmes (1863–1942), Swarthmore College philosophy professor, one of the founders of the American Friends Service Committee and clerk of Progressive Friends Meeting at Longwood. He was also a radio talk show host who ran for governor of Pennsylvania as a Socialist. A memoir about Holmes and a full biography have been published.[62]

In 1928 Jesse Holmes published a letter titled "To the Scientifically-Minded" in *Friends Intelligencer*. A slightly shorter version was published by Friends General Conference signed by Jesse Holmes and five other Quaker professors: Paul H. Douglas, Thomas A. Jenkins, Albert T. Mills, J. Russell Smith, and Roscoe Pound. FGC distributed 20,000 copies in English and Spanish and it appeared in *Atlantic*, *Christian Century*, *Harpers*, and *Unity*, and was mentioned in *Time*.[63] Holmes wrote, "We Friends . . . have a faith . . . which has nothing to fear from science and which demands no medieval credulities of intelligent people. We invite such people to examine our faith and see if they do not belong with us."[64] Three years later he wrote,

It has not often been, and should never be, that knowledge of truth as revealed to the scientist, is out of place in our galleries. Certainly that vision of what should be which in all ages is the heart of religion, must be based on what is now, or our temple will lack foundation and be no more than a castle in the air. The spirit of the Society of Friends is closely allied to the spirit of the genuine scientists. It involves that intimate relation between ourselves and our world which makes any final statement of it in a formula impossible. . . . I believe a very large and increasing number of the scientists of the world are in unity with the essential Quaker point of view.[65]

There are many steps we can take. We can invite Friends to write about science and Quakers from our many different perspectives. We can continue the study of ways to be diverse religious communities. The story of Friends in science, past and present, can be a topic in our schools. Quaker scientists and artists can cooperate on projects. We can support monthly meetings in studying specific environmental issues and the general relation of Quakers and science.

It will help if Friends mention religious diversity in our visitor brochures. This can be as simple as the two sentences that were added as a footnote to the QEW Vision & Witness webpage: "Some Friends may choose different language to describe their personal reasons for supporting or sharing in the work of Quaker Earthcare Witness. All are welcome who seek to further QEW's programs and activities." A longer statement about this has been approved by the QEW Spiritual Nurturance Committee and is on their website. (See page 102, below.)[66]

It will also help if we make clear to each other and to newcomers that individual seekers in local meeting communities are the heart of our faith; that we ask each person to interpret statements approved by the group as we do statements of individuals; that unity in our community is a sign of participation and commitment; and that we endeavor to love each other beliefs and all.

Scientists can be Quakers. Many have found a congenial religious home among Friends. Quakers will benefit from their expertise, and their participation in our communities. I hope Quakers will reach out to scientists and encourage them to visit us.

History

We, even we, as small and as contemptible as we are in ourselves, yet we are members of the Sea; poor drops though we be, yet let us not be discouraged: We belong to the vast Ocean.

—John Everard (p. 118)

A note about
Roots and Flowers of Quaker Nontheism

In 2003 I saw Esther Greenleaf Mürer's pamphlet, Beyond Uneasy Tolerance, *a collection of excerpts from Quaker writing about Friends and the arts showing the gradual acceptance of what was once forbidden.* Clearly, the same could be done for people who have written about Quakerism from a naturalistic, or relatively naturalistic, perspective.*

I started looking for writings by Quaker theological skeptics and Friends who advocated views that later made it possible for Quakers to be philosophical naturalists. This led to Roots and Flowers of Quaker Nontheism.

Many Friends helped, including Robin Alpern, David Boulton, Joan Lukas, James Riemermann, and David and Kitty Rush. Chuck Fager urged me on, not deterred by the differences in our personal views. Librarians were generous with time, knowledge, and enthusiasm at Haverford and Swarthmore Colleges and in Burlington County, New Jersey, and Iowa City, Iowa.

---

*Esther Greenleaf Mürer, ed., *Beyond Uneasy Tolerance: The saga of Quakers and the arts in 100 quotations* (Philadelphia PA: Fellowship of Quakers in the Arts, 2000).

Roots and Flowers of Quaker Nontheism

Part I: Roots of Quaker Nontheism

This is a study of the roots of Quaker nontheism today. Nontheist Friends are powerfully drawn to Quaker practices but they do not accompany this with a faith in God. Nontheism is an umbrella term covering atheists, agnostics, secular humanists, pantheists, wiccaists, and others. You can combine nontheist with other terms and call yourself an agnostic nontheist or atheist nontheist, and so on. Some nontheists have set aside one version of God (e.g. as a person) and not another (e.g. as a word for good or your highest values). A negative term like nontheism is convenient because we describe our views so many different ways when speaking positively.

Many of the Quakers mentioned here were not nontheists but are included because they held views, often heretical in their time, that helped Friends become more inclusive. In the early days this included questioning the divinity of Christ, the divine inspiration of the Bible, and the concepts of heaven, hell, and immortality. Later Friends questioned miracles, the trinity, and divine creation. Recently the issue has been whether Quakers have to be Christians, or theists. All this time there were other changes happening in speech, clothing, marriage practices, and so on. Quakerism has always been in progress.

Views held today are no more authentic because they were present in some form in earlier years. However, it is encouraging to Quaker nontheists today to find their views and their struggle prefigured among Friends of an earlier day.

In the following excerpts we learn about Quaker skeptics of the past and the issues they stood for. These are the roots that support the flowers of contemporary Quaker nontheism. (A bibliography of resource materials for these people is in the Appendix on p. 147, below.)

First Generation Quaker Skeptics

Quakers were a varied group at the beginning. There was little effective doctrinal control and individuals were encouraged to think for themselves within the contexts of their local meetings. Many of the early traditions are key for nontheists today, such as the emphasis on actions other than talk and the injunction to interpret what we read, even Scripture. All the early Friends can be considered forerunners of the Quaker nontheists of today, but two people deserve special mention. **Gerard Winstanley** (1609–c.1660) was a Digger, or True Leveller, who became a Quaker. (For other excerpts, see pp. 107, 117, 118, 120 & 122.) He published twenty pamphlets between 1648 and 1652 and was a political and religious revolutionary. He equated God with the law of the universe known by observation and reason guided by conscience and love. Winstanley wrote,

> I'll appeal to your self in this question, what other knowledge have you of God but what you have within the circle of the creation?... For if the creation in all its dimensions be the fullness of him that fills all with himself, and if you yourself be part of this creation, where can you find God but in that line or station wherein you stand.[67]

Winstanley also wrote,

> [T]he Spirit Reason, which I call God...is that spirituall power, that guids all mens reasoning in right order, and to a right end: for the Spirit Reason, doth not preserve one creature and destroy another.... but it hath a regard to the whole creation; and knits every creature together into a onenesse; making every creature to be an upholder of his fellow.[68]

His emphasis was on the world around and within us: "O ye hear-say Preachers, deceive not the people any longer, by telling them that this glory shal not be known and seen, til the body is laid in the dust. I tel you, this great mystery is begun to appear, and it must be seen by the material eyes of the flesh: And those five senses that is in man, shall partake of this glory."[69]

Jacob Bauthumley (1613–1692) was a shoemaker who served in the Parliamentary Army. (For another excerpt, see p. 106.) His name was probably pronounced Bottomley since this is how Fox spelled it. In 1650 he published *The Light and Dark Sides of God,* the only pamphlet of his that we have. This was declared blasphemous and he was thrown out of the army, his sword broken over his head, and his tongue bored. After the Restoration he became a Quaker and a librarian and was elected sergeant-at-mace in Leicester. For Bauthumley, God dwells in men and in all the rest of creation and nowhere else. We are God even when we sin. Jesus was no more divine than any person is, and the Bible is not the word of God. He wrote,

I see that all the Beings in the World are but that one Being, and so he may well be said, to be every where as he is, and so I cannot exclude him from Man or Beast, or any other Creature: Every Creature and thing having that Being living in it, and there is no difference betwixt Man and Beast; but as Man carries a more lively Image of the divine Being then [than] any other Creature: For I see the Power, Wisdom, and Glory of God in one, as well as another onely in that Creature called Man, God appears more gloriously in then the rest. . . . And God loves the Being of all Creatures, yea, all men are alike to him, and have received lively impressions of the divine nature, though they be not so gloriously and purely manifested in some as in others, some live in the light side of God, and some in the dark side; But in respect of God, light and darkness are all one to him; for there is nothing contrary to God, but onely to our apprehension. . . . It is not so safe to go to the Bible to see what others have spoken and writ of the mind of God as to see what God speaks within me and to follow the doctrine and leadings of it in me.[70]

Eighteenth Century Quaker Skeptics

There were skeptical Quakers who asserted views such as that God created but does not run the universe, that Jesus was a man and not divine, that much of theology is superstition and divides people unnecessarily, and that the soul is mortal.

An example is **John Bartram** (1699–1777) of Philadelphia. (For another excerpt, see p. 117.) He was a farmer and perhaps the best known botanist in the American colonies. Bartram had a mystical feeling for the presence of God in nature and he supported the rational study of nature. In 1758 he was disowned by Darby Meeting for saying Jesus was not divine, but he continued to worship at that meeting and was buried there.

In 1761 he carved a quote from Alexander Pope over the door of his greenhouse: "Slave to no sect, who takes no private road, but looks through Nature up to Nature's God." In 1743 he wrote, "When we are upon the topic of astrology, magic and mystic divinity, I am apt to be a little troublesome, by inquiring into the foundation and reasonableness of these notions." In a letter to Benjamin Rush he wrote, "I hope a more diligent search will lead you into the knowledge of more certain truths than all the pretended revelations of our mystery mongers and their inspirations."[71]

Here is how Bartram described the flowers he saw:

> What charming colours appear in the various tribes! What a glow is enkindled in some! What a gloss shines in others! With what a masterly skill is every one of the varying tints disposed! Here they seem to be thrown on with an easy freedom, there they are adjusted with the nicest touches. Some are intersected with elegant stripes, or studded with radiant spots; others affect to be genteelly powdered, or neatly fringed. Some are arrayed in purple; some charm with the virgin's white; others are dashed with crim-

son; while others are robed in scarlet. Some glitter like silver lace; others shine as if embroidered with gold.[72]

Bartram's sons, Moses, John, and James, were founding members of the Free Quakers.

Free Quakers

These Friends were disowned for abandoning the peace testimony during the Revolutionary War. The Free Quakers cast the issue in more general terms. They supported freedom of conscience and saw themselves as upholding the original Friends' traditions. They wrote:

> We have no new doctrine to teach, nor any design of promoting schisms in religion. We wish only to be freed from every species of ecclesiastical tyranny, and mean to pay a due regard to the principles of our forefathers . . . and hope, thereby, to preserve decency and to secure equal liberty to all. We have no designs to form creeds or confessions of faith, but [hope] to leave every man to think and judge for himself . . . and to answer for his faith and opinions to . . . the sole Judge and sovereign Lord of conscience.[73]

Their discipline forbade all forms of disownment: "Neither shall a member be deprived of his right among us, on account of his differing in sentiment from any or all of his brethren."[74]

There were several Free Quaker meetings, the longest lasting being the one in Philadelphia from 1781 to 1834.

Proto-Hicksites

Some the views that emerged during the schism of 1827 had been expressed much earlier. **Job Scott** (1751–1793) saw all outward signs, such as the Bible, creeds, reason, and learning, as hindrance to the experience of the inward Christ. His *Journal*, published in 1797, aroused opposition from evangelical Christians.

There were also the New Lights in Ireland. **Abraham Shackleton** (1752–1818) emphasized the experience of the Inner Light and objected to legalistic disciplines and scriptural doctrine. He was disowned in 1801.

Hannah Barnard (1754–1825) of New York questioned the interpretation of events in the Bible and put reason above orthodoxy and ethics over theology. She wrote a manual in the form of a dialogue to teach domestic science to rural women. It included philosophy, civics, and autobiography. Barnard supported the French Revolution and insisted that masters and servants sit together during her visits. In 1802 she was silenced as a minister and disowned by Friends. She wrote,

> [N]othing is revealed truth to me, as doctrine, until it is sealed as such on the mind, through the illumination of that uncreated word of God, or divine light, and intelligence, to which the Scriptures, as well as the writings of many other enlightened authors, of different ages, bear plentiful testimony. . . . I therefore do not attach the idea or title of divine infallibility to any society as such, or to any book, or books, in the world; but to the great source of eternal truth only.[75]

Barnard also wrote, "under the present state of the Society I can with humble reverent thankfulness rejoice in the consideration that I was made the Instrument of bringing their Darkness to light."[76] On hearing Elias Hicks in 1819, she is said to have commented that these were the ideas for which she had been disowned. He visited her in 1824, a year before she died.

In Massachusetts there was a group called the New Lights that included **Mary Newhall** (c.1780–1829) and **Mary Rotch**. They opposed the power of the Elders, sometimes theatrically by occupying the facing benches or wearing bright colors to meeting. They held reason and individual perception of truth over the authority of Scripture. These New Lights expressed views similar to those of

Abraham Shackleton, Hannah Barnard, and Elias Hicks. About sixty Friends were disowned and the movement died out. The dissenters did not continue meeting together and many became Unitarians. Ralph Waldo Emerson spoke highly of them. In the Hicksite-Orthodox schism of 1827, New England Yearly Meeting did not divide and one reason for this may be that they had already confronted and disowned the New Lights.

Hicksites

The schism that started in 1827 involved many people but it is instructive to focus on one man at the center of the conflict. **Elias Hicks** (1748–1830) traveled widely, urging Friends to follow a God known inwardly and to resist the domination of others in the Society. He wrote,

> There is scarcely anything so baneful to the present and future happiness and welfare of mankind, as a submission to traditional and popular opinion, I have therefore been led to see the necessity of investigating for myself all customs and doctrines . . . either verbally or historically communicated . . . and not to sit down satisfied with any thing but the plain, clear, demonstrative testimony of the spirit and word of life and light in my heart and conscience.[77]

Hicks emphasized the inward action of the Spirit rather than human effort or learning, but he saw a place for reason. He turned to "the light in our own consciences, . . . the reason of things, . . . the precepts and example of our Lord Jesus Christ, (and) the golden rule."[78]

A proponent of Hicks's views was **Benjamin Ferris** (1780–1867), editor of *The Berean*, and the first Clerk of the Hicksite yearly meeting in Philadelphia. He rejected creedal doctrine and claimed Inner Light sufficient for salvation of any person. He emphasized historical relativism and grounded his religion on facts and evidence rather than mystery and emotion. In 1821–1823 he published a debate with an evangelical minister, *Letters of Paul and Amicus*, which contributed to the schism in 1827.

Manchester Free Friends

David Duncan (c.1825–1871), a former Presbyterian who had trained for the ministry, was a merchant and manufacturer in Manchester, England. He married **Sarah Ann Cooke Duncan** and became a Friend in 1852. He was a republican, a social radical, a Free Thinker, and an aggressive writer and debater. Duncan began to doubt Quaker views about God and the Bible and associated the Light Within with intellectual freedom. He developed a following at the Friends Institute in Manchester and the publication of his *Essays and Reviews* in 1861 brought the attention of the Elders. In it he wrote, "If the principle were more generally admitted that Christianity is a life rather than a formula, theology would give place to religion . . . and that peculiarly bitter spirit which actuates religionists would no longer be associated with the profession of religion."[70] In 1871 he was disowned and then died suddenly of smallpox. Sarah Ann Duncan and about 14 others resigned from their meeting and started what came to be called the Free Friends.

In 1873, this group approved a statement which included the following:

> It is now more than two years and a quarter since we sought, outside of the Society of Friends, for the liberty to speak the thoughts and convictions we entertained which was denied to us within its borders, and for the enjoyment of the privilege of companionship in "unity of spirit," without the limitations imposed upon it by forced identity of opinion on the obscure propositions of theologians. We were told that such unity could not be practically obtained along with diversity of sentiment upon fundamental questions, but we did not see that this need necessarily be true where a principle of cohesion was assented to which involved tolerance to all opinions; and we therefore determined ourselves to try the experiment, and

so remove the question, if possible, out of the region of speculation into that of practice. We conceived one idea in common, with great diversity of opinion amongst us, upon all the questions which divide men in their opinions of the government and constitution of the universe. We felt that whatever was true was better for us than that which was not, and that we attained it best by listening and thinking for ourselves.[80]

Joseph B. Forster (1831–1883) was a leader of the dissidents after the death of David Duncan. (For another excerpt, see pp. 17.) He wrote, "[E]very law which fixes a limit to free thought, exists in violation of the very first of all doctrines held by the Early Quakers,—the doctrine of the 'Inner Light'."[81]

Forster was editor of a journal published by the Free Friends. In the first issue he wrote,

> We ask for [The Manchester Friend] the support of those who, with widely divergent opinions, are united in the belief that dogma is not religion, and that truth can only be made possible to us where perfect liberty of thought is conceded. We ask for it also the support of those, who, recognizing this, feel that Christianity is a *life* and not a creed; and that obedience to our knowledge of what is pure and good is the end of all religion. We may fall below our ideal, but we shall try not to do so; and we trust our readers will, as far as they can, aid us in our task.[82]

He also wrote, "Thus, knowledge, the handmaid of religion, lays the foundations of faith, and gives man hope: revealing dimly to the imagination the wealth which lies buried in the ocean, beyond the shore on which we stand, it adds to our confidence in an infinite of goodness, before which we rationally and reverently bow."[83]

In the last issue of the journal Forster wrote,

> The sole object of the *Manchester Friend* has been to ask men to

be perfectly ingenuous in the expression of all they believe or disbelieve, on every question sufficiently interesting to have made them think, and to teach them to *listen*, and to remember, as they do so, that God has not furnished the world with any infallible Pope, either at Rome, in the shape of a Quaker's Meeting of Ministers and Elders, or in any other form.[84]

George S. Brady (1833–1913) was a scientist, a member of the Royal Society of London, and a supporter of Charles Darwin. Brady published opinion pieces in *The Manchester Friend*. In 1873 he wrote,

(U)nless this Society shows in coming years more capacity to discern the signs of the times than it has recently shown, unless it can be brought to see that religious belief . . . must advance with . . . advancing knowledge, it will inevitably fall back, even further than it has already fallen, from its old position in the advanced guard of religious freedom.[85]

In his *Essay on the Exercise of the Intellect in Matters of Religious Belief,* Brady called for biblical criticism, reconciliation with science, and freedom of conscience.

George Brady and the other Free Friends were thirty years ahead of their yearly meeting which created difficulties for all concerned but was important for the evolution of our Society.[86]

Progressive and Congregational Friends

The Progressive Friends at Longwood (near Philadelphia) were committed to peace, and the rights of women and blacks, and were also concerned about church governance and doctrine. (For another excerpt, see p. 15.) Between 1844 and 1874 they separated from other Hicksite Quakers and formed a monthly meeting and a yearly meeting. They asked, "What right had one Friend, or one group of Friends, to judge the leadings of others?"[87] They objected to partitions between men's and women's meetings and the authority of meeting elders and ministers over the expression of individual conscience and other actions of the members. There were similar separations in Indiana Yearly Meeting (Orthodox) in the 1840s, Green Plain Quarterly Meeting in Ohio in 1843 and in Genesee Yearly Meeting (Hicksite) in northern New York and Michigan and in New York Yearly Meeting in 1846 and 1848.

A Congregational Friend in New York declared,

> We do not require that persons shall believe that the Bible is an inspired book; we do not even demand that they shall have an unwavering faith in their own immortality; nor do we require them to assert a belief in the existence of God. We do not catechize men at all as to their theological opinions. Our only test is one which applies to the heart, not to the head. To all who seek truth we extend the hand of fellowship, without distinction of sex, creed and color. We open our doors, to all who wish to unite with us in promoting peace and good will among men. We ask all who are striving to elevate humanity to come here and stand with us on equal terms.[88]

In their *Basis of Religious Association* Progressive Friends at Longwood welcomed "all who acknowledge the duty of defining and illustrating their faith in God, not by assent to a creed, but lives of personal purity, and works of beneficence and charity to mankind." They also wrote,

> We seek not to diminish, but to intensify in ourselves the sense of individual responsibility. . . . We have set forth no forms or ceremonies; nor have we sought to impose upon ourselves or others a system of doctrinal belief. Such matters we have left where Jesus left them, with the conscience and common sense of the individual. It has been our cherished purpose to restore the union between religion and life, and to place works of goodness and mercy far above theological speculations and scholastic subtleties of

doctrine. Creed-making is not among the objects of our association. Christianity, as it presents itself to our minds, is too deep, too broad, and too high to be brought within the cold propositions of the theologian. We should as soon think of bottling up the sunshine for the use of posterity, as of attempting to adjust the free and universal principles taught and exemplified by Jesus of Nazareth to the angles of a manmade creed.[89]

Between 1863 and 1874 many of the Friends at Longwood were taken back into membership by their meetings. By the time of the birth of modern liberal Quakerism at the turn of the century, many Friends in unprogrammed meetings had become progressives.

Quaker Free Thinkers

Liberal religious dissenters in the nineteenth century were called Free Thinkers. **Lucretia Mott** (1793–1880) worked for abolition of slavery, women's suffrage, and temperance. (For another excerpt, see p. 119.) Her motto was "Truth for authority, and not authority for truth." She refused to be controlled by her meeting but also refused to leave it. Her meeting denied permission to travel in the ministry after 1843 but she went anyway. Mott was a founding member of the Free Religious Association in 1867, when she told them, "I believe that such proving all things, such trying all things, and holding fast only to that which is good, is the great religious duty of our age. . . . Our own conscience and the Divine Spirit's teaching are always harmonious and this Divine illumination is as freely given to man as his reason, or as are many of his natural powers." She also said, "I confess to great skepticism as to any account or story, which conflicts with the unvarying natural laws of God in his creation."[90]

In 1840 Elizabeth Fry refused to shake Lucretia Mott's hand because of her Hicksite and Unitarian views. In 1849 Mott said,

I confess to you, my friends, that I am a worshipper after the way called heresy—a believer after the manner many deem infidel.

While at the same time my faith is firm in the blessed, the eternal doctrine preached by Jesus and by every child of God since the creation of the world, especially the great truth that God is the teacher of his people himself; the doctrine that Jesus most emphatically taught, that the kingdom is with man, that there is his sacred and divine temple.[91]

On another occasion she said, "Men are too superstitious, too prone to believe what is presented to them by their church and creed; they ought to follow Jesus more in his non-conformity. . . . I hold that skepticism is a religious duty; men should question their theology and doubt more in order that they might believe more."[92]

Elizabeth Cady Stanton wrote in her diary that Mott said to her,

There is a broad distinction between religion and theology. The one is a natural, human experience common to all well-organized minds. The other is a system of speculations about the unseen and the unknowable, which the human mind has no power to grasp or explain, and these speculations vary with every sect, age, and type of civilization. No one knows any more of what lies beyond our sphere of action than thou and I, and we know nothing.[93]

Maria Mitchell (1818–1889), a Friend who became a Unitarian, was an astronomer, professor at Vassar College, founder of the American Association for the Advancement of Women, and first woman elected to the American Association for the Advancement of Science, the American Philosophical Society, and the American Academy of Arts and Sciences. Mitchell wrote in her diary (all the following quotes are from the privacy of her diary), "It seems to me that if anything would make me an infidel, it would be the threats lavished against unbelief." Later, she wrote, "Why cannot a man act himself, be himself, and think for himself? It seems to me that naturalness alone is power; that a borrowed word is weaker than our own weakness, however small we may be. If I reach a girl's heart or head, I know I must reach it through my own, and not from bigger hearts and heads than mine." Mitchell also wrote, "(Resolved) . . . If possible, connect myself with liberal Christian institutions, believing as I do that happiness and growth in this life are best promoted by them and that what is good in this life is good in any life."[94]

She saw no conflict between religion and science, and she defended Charles Darwin's theory of evolution:

> Can the study of *truth* do harm? Does not every true scientist seek only to know the truth? And in our deep ignorance of what is truth, shall we dread the searching after it? I hold the simple student of nature in holy reverence and . . . I cannot bear to have these sincere workers held up in the least degree to reproach. And let us have *truth* even if the truth be the awful denial of the good God. We must face the light and not bury our heads in the Earth.[95]

Another Free Thinker was **Susan B. Anthony** (1820–1906). She was an active supporter of rights for women, abolition of slavery, and temperance. Raised a Quaker, she considered herself one even after she joined the Unitarians because her meeting failed to support abolition. Her friend, Elizabeth Cady Stanton, called her an agnostic. She refused to express her opinion on religious subjects, saying she could only work on one reform at a time. In 1890 she told a women's organization, "These are the principles I want to maintain—that our platform may be kept as broad as the universe, that upon it may stand the representatives of all creeds and of no creeds—Jew and Christian, Protestant and Catholic, Gentile and Mormon, believer and atheist." In a speech in 1896 she said, "I distrust those people who know so well what God wants them to do, because I notice it always coincides with their own desires. . . . What you should say to outsiders is that a Christian has neither more nor less rights in our association than an atheist. When our platform becomes too narrow for people of all creeds and of no creeds, I myself can not stand upon it." When asked in an interview in 1896 "Do you pray?", she answered, "I pray every single second of my life; not on my knees, but with my work. My prayer is to lift women to equality with men. Work and worship are one with me. I know there is no God of the universe made happy by my getting down on my knees and calling him 'great'." In 1897 she wrote, "(I)t does not matter whether it is Calvinism, Unitarianism, Spiritualism, Christian Science, or Theosophy, they are all speculations. So I think you and I had better hang on to this mundane sphere and keep tugging away to make conditions better for the next generation of women." Anthony said to a group of Quakers in 1885, "I don't know what religion is. I only know what work is, and that is all I can speak on, this side of Jordan."[96]

Elizabeth Cady Stanton (1815–1902) was a leader of the women's suffrage movement for fifty-five years and one of the most famous and outspoken Free Thinkers of her day. She was a member of Junius Monthly Meeting, a Congregational meeting in upstate New York, during their first ten years after splitting off from Genesee Yearly Meeting in 1848. As a child she was terrified by preaching about human depravity and sinners' damnation. Later she wrote, "My religious superstitions gave place to rational ideas based on scientific facts, and in proportion, as I looked at everything from a new standpoint, I grew more happy day by day."[97] She also wrote,

> I can say that the happiest period of my life has been since I emerged from the shadows and superstitions of the old theologies, relieved from all gloomy apprehensions of the future, satisfied that as my labors and capacities were limited to this sphere of action, I was responsible for nothing beyond my horizon, as I could neither understand nor change the condition of the unknown world. Giving ourselves, then, no trouble about the future, let us make the most of the present, and fill up our lives with earnest work here.[98]

Stanton led a committee that produced the *Woman's Bible* which removed the parts that called for the domination of women by men. She wrote, "When women understand that governments and religions are human inventions; that bibles, prayerbooks, catechisms, and encyclical letters are all emanations from the brain of man, they will no longer be oppressed by the injunctions that come to them with the divine authority of 'thus saith the Lord.'" Stanton also wrote, "I have endeavored to dissipate these religious superstitions from the minds of women and base their faith on science and reason, where I found for myself at lat that peace and comfort I could never find in the Bible and church."[99]

Modern Liberal Friends

Edward T. Bennett (1831–1908) was the last Quaker disowned for heresy by the Yearly Meeting in Britain (in 1873). A new liberal consensus began to form with the publication in London in 1884 of *A Reasonable Faith: Short Essays for the Times by Three 'Friends'*, written by anonymous authors who later turned out to be **Francis Frith** (1822–1898), **William Pollard** (1828–1893), and **William E. Turner** (1836–1911).

Joseph Rowntree (1836–1925) was a chocolate manufacturer and reformer of the Religious Society of Friends and of society in general. He helped craft the London Yearly Meeting response to the Richmond Declaration of 1887, when he wrote, "(T)he general welfare of the Society of Friends the world over will not be advanced by one Yearly Meeting following exactly in the footsteps of another, but by each being faithful to its own convictions and experience. This may not result in a rigid uniformity of either thought or action, but it is likely to lead to something far better—to a true and living unity."[100]

The conference of Friends in Manchester in 1895 was a clear declaration of their views, as was the first Summer School (on the British model) at Haverford College in 1900, the founding of Friends General Conference in 1900 and American Friends Service Committee in 1917.

William Littleboy (c.1852–1936) and wife **Margaret Littleboy** were among the first staff at Woodbrooke Quaker Study Centre. William Littleboy was an advocate of ethical living as basis for religion, and of opening the Religious Society of Friends to skeptics. In 1902 he wrote to Rufus Jones urging consideration be given to Quakers who do not have mystical experiences, and in 1916 he published a pamphlet, *The Appeal of Quakerism to the Non-Mystic*. In it he wrote,

> We know that to some choice souls God's messages come in ways which are super-normal, and it is natural that we should look with longing eyes on these; yet such cases are the exception, not the rule. . . . Let us then take ourselves at our best. [Non-mystics] *are* capable of thought and care for others. We *do* at times abase ourselves that others may be exalted. On occasion we succeed in loving our enemies and doing good to those who despitefully use us. For those who are nearest to us we would suffer—perhaps even give our life, because we love them so. . . . To the great non-mystic majority [the Quaker's] appeal should come with special power, for he can speak to them, as none other can whose gospel is less universal.[101]

This influenced the young Henry Cadbury who many years later said, "I am sure that over the years [William Littleboy's] perceptive presentation of the matter has brought real relief to many of us."[102]

Arthur Stanley Eddington (1882–1934), an astronomer, felt that scientists and Quakers had something important in common. In 1930 he wrote,

> I think that the spirit of seeking is still the prevailing one in our [Quaker] faith, which for that reason is not embodied in any creed or formula. . . . The finding of one generation will not serve the next. It tarnishes rapidly except it be preserved with an ever-renewed spirit of seeking. . . . Religious creeds are a great obstacle to any full sympathy between the outlook of the scientist and the outlook which religion is so often supposed to require. . . . But I think it may be said that Quakerism in dispensing with creeds holds out a hand to the scientist.[103]

Joel Bean (1825–1914) and **Hannah Shipley Bean** (1830–1909) were attracted to older forms of Quaker worship instead of pastors and revivals. In 1887 they founded the College Park Association in California, prototype for new unprogrammed meetings. They were open to new thought and were less concerned with doctrinal agreement. They were disowned by Iowa Yearly Meeting in 1892.

Reunifiers

Some Friends worked their entire lives to bring together dissident branches of the Religious Society of Friends. Examples are **Henry Cadbury** and **Rufus Jones**. They based their call for reunification on the same grounds that nontheist Friends rely on today. These included an emphasis on practice rather than beliefs; the idea that Quakers need not hold the same beliefs; describing Quaker beliefs in the meeting discipline by quoting from the writings of individuals; the idea that religiously inspired action can be associated with many different faiths; the love of diversity within the Religious Society of Friends; the view that religion is a matter our daily lives; and the emphasis on Jesus as a person rather than doctrine about Jesus.

These bases for reunification among Friends also serve to include nonmystics, nonChristians, and people of other faiths including nontheist faiths.

NonChristian Friends

At regular intervals during the history of Friends there is discussion about whether we have to be Christian to be Quaker. This is often in the form of an exchange of letters in a Quaker journal. One such flurry was prompted by two letters from **Watchman** in *The Friend* in 1943 and 1944 (reprinted in 1994).

In 1953 **Arthur Morgan** proposed inviting people of other faiths to join Friends (see page 87). In 1966 **Henry Cadbury** was asked to address the question in a talk given at the annual sessions of Pacific Yearly Meeting. In his view Quakerism and Christianity represent sets of beliefs from which individuals make selections, with no one belief required of all (see page 20). Quaker universalists have raised the issue many times (for example, **John Linton** in 1979 and **Daniel A. Seeger** in 1984).[104]

Universalist Friends

The Quaker Universalist Group was formed in Britain in 1979, and the Quaker Universalist Fellowship in the United States in 1983. Among the founders were nontheists **John Linton** and **Kingdon W. Swayne**. It is a diverse movement. For the early Friends universalism meant that any person could be saved by Christ. Today, for some Friends universalism is about accepting diversity of religious faith. For others it is an active searching for common aspects of different faiths. Universalism can also mean an effort to learn from each other and live together well and love each other, differences and all.

Conclusion

Over the years, many Quakers stood against the doctrinal views of their times. They represent a continual stream of dissent and a struggle for inclusiveness that started with the birth of our Society. What was rejected at one point was accepted later. Much of what Friends believe today would have been heresy in the past.

Through the years, certain traditions in the Religious Society of Friends have supported the presence of doctrinal skeptics. This included being noncreedal, tolerant, and universalist; concern for experience rather than beliefs; authority of the individual as well as the community, interpreting what we read; and the conviction that Quaker practice and Quaker membership do not require agreement on religious doctrine.

Many Quaker practices are typically explained in terms of God, Spirit or the Inner Light, such as worship, leadings, discernment, the sense of the meeting, and continual revelation. Nontheist Friends embrace the practices without the explanation.

Part II: Flowers Of Quaker Nontheism

This is a look at Quaker nontheism flowering today. Nontheist Friends, by and large, do not experience, accept or believe in a deity. As a negatively defined term, nontheism provides a broad tent for people who hold many different positive views.

In general, nontheists support diversity of thought in the Religious Society of Friends. They bless what theists and nontheists bring to their meetings and the opportunities that come with diversity. They have been cautious about forming their own organizations because they want to join rather than separate from theist Friends. They hope we will accept each other as Quakers, without adjectives.

The material gathered here represents the flowering of Quaker nontheism.

Proto-Nontheist Friends

These Friends were humanists who showed a tender concern for religious skeptics but they did not publicly address the issue of nontheism. We do not know what their personal views were (or are) and it doesn't matter. It is enough that they helped create the Religious Society of Friends of today that includes meetings that welcome nontheists.

Jesse Herman Holmes (1863–1942) was a passionate advocate for Quakerism free of creeds. (For more on Holmes and other excerpts, see pp. 31 & 60.) In 1928 in "To the Scientifically-Minded" he wrote, "[Friends] have no common creed, and such unity—of which there is a great deal—as there is among them is merely due to the fact that impartial minds, working on the same conditions, arrive at similar conclusions. However, we demand no unity of opinion, but find interest and stimulus in our many differences."[105]

Holmes did not see religion as establishing truth. He wrote in 1912: "The accurate formulating of our ends and of the tested ways of attaining them is the function of philosophy and the sciences. The more difficult task of holding ourselves to the higher loyalties is that of religion. Not the discovery of truth but the patient using of it for the more abundant life is its task." He saw that Friends can provide a congenial home for scientists, and in fact we need them.[106]

In private Jesse Holmes could be outspoken. In a manuscript that was not published until 61 years after his death, he wrote:

> Meaningless phrases and irrational theologies have been moulded into rigid, authoritative institutions perverting and stultifying the adventurous, creative spirit which distinguishes us from the rest of the animal kingdom. They turn our attention from the splendid possibilities of our mysterious life and toward a mythical, improbable life after death. Over all presides a despotic, unjust, and irrational deity of the medieval king type, who must be worshipped by flattery and blind obedience. . . . I propose to a fairly intelligent people of a partially scientific age . . . that all this is a sad mess of ancient and medieval superstition which should speedily be relegated to the storage rooms of the museum of history. We should stop the pretense of awe, or even respect, for teachings which lack even a slight amount of evidence or probability. We should substitute a religion based on actual repeatable, describable and testable experience, and which has some connection with the genuine values of life: not an absurd and impossible life in a stupid, idle heaven, but a rich, active, adventurous life in the world we live in. . . . [I]f those who reject all this medieval rubbish will join heartily in a real world-wide effort for an uplifted humanity; if they refuse to continue systems which involve contests in indiscriminate killing and destruction; if they will dedicate themselves to a general cooperation in mutual service, refusing all incitements to seek power over each other; if they will accept the adventure of lives everywhere seeking harmony, good-will, understanding, friendliness; if they will turn aside from all claims of super-men for super-rights and privileges, whether in religion, in politics, in industry or in society; then indeed we may renew and revive the purposes of prophets, statesmen, scholars, scientists, and good people since the world began. This would be a real religion.[107]

Henry Joel Cadbury (1883–1974) was an outspoken advocate for a variety of Quakerism without mysticism, unity based on love rather than dogma, beliefs as collateral effects rather than sources of action, ethical living as religion, and the possibility of life as spontaneous response to passing situations. (For other excerpts, see pp. 20, 22, 49, 54, 81, 101, & 121.) He worked his entire life for unity among Friends. He was an historian of the Religious Society of Friends, a Biblical scholar, a social activist, and a humorist. Cadbury hid his personal beliefs, preferring to help others find their way. He did lift the veil once when he wrote a manuscript that he apparently read to his divinity students in 1936. (It was not published until 2000.) He stated,

> I can describe myself as no ardent theist or atheist. . . . My own religion is mainly neither emotional nor rational but expresses itself habitually or occasionally in action. . . . If you know John Woolman's Journal you will know what I mean by a religious personality in action. . . . The amazing revelation which he gives is that of a sensitive conscience feeling its course in a series of soul-searching problems—public problems that he felt must be personally decided. Such forms of religion do not often get recorded, but they are none the less real and important. . . . And what is the real test or evidence of religion that I can offer in myself? . . . It is whether in all our contacts . . . you can conclude that not consciously nor for display I represent the manner of reaction that befits a religious personality in action.[108]

In the Swarthmore Lecture in 1957, recalling how helpful it had been to read William Littleboy's *The Appeal of Quakerism to the Non-Mystic*, Cadbury said,

> Someone ought to write a pamphlet *The Appeal of Quakerism to the Non-Theological* to help them with their inferiority complex. . . . They seem to others and perhaps to themselves subject to some defect. Perhaps it is intellectual laziness, or some con-

genital skepticism. . . . The repetitious recourse to any doctrinal framework, including the one most in fashion in the Society at the time, they do not find helpful to themselves, and they regard it as perhaps their duty and privilege to seek for or to exemplify other aspects of truth to supplement the limited emphasis. It is not that they wish to deny what the theologian affirms, but that they find his approach uncongenial and irrelevant to their own spiritual life, and they are indifferent or even pained or estranged when it is made central in the definition of Quakerism. . . . It does not speak to their condition. Their search is not for a more satisfactory theology, they do not believe that for them spiritual progress depends upon such factors. The obscurity of the mysteries of God does not really bother them and they have no confidence that even the most rational of religious analyses would add a cubit to their moral stature. They have, therefore, neither the will nor the competence to deal with the situation, but they hold their peace by simply keeping their own counsels without contradiction or controversy.[109]

Arthur Morgan (1878–1975) was an engineer, educator, and utopian. (For another excerpt, see p. 18.) He was president of Antioch College, chairman and chief engineer of the Tennessee Valley Authority, a founder of Celo Community and the Fellowship of Intentional Communities. He was a Unitarian who became a Friend in 1940. In 1953 Morgan proposed a minute to his yearly meeting opening Friends membership to people of other faiths. In it he stated,

Many men and women of many faiths have shared in the search for truth and love and human brotherhood. Each faith has helped its sincere followers in that search. Each faith has something to learn from the others, and something to give. The Lake Erie Association of Friends desires to be a unit of such a brotherhood, and welcomes into its membership and to its meetings all sincere, concerned seekers whose ways of life and ethical standards and practices are compatible with its own.[110]

The minute was not approved.

Arthur Morgan declined to sign the Humanist Manifesto in 1933. He saw positive value in religion and did not want it cast aside. In a letter published in the same issue of *The New Humanist* as the manifesto, he wrote:

> I believe that unless the Humanist movement achieves a better distribution of emphasis, it will act as a sectarian movement to divide those who have one partial view of the issues of life from those who have another partial view . . . [A]ny vital religion must give great emphasis to faith, which in essence is an unproven conviction of the significance of living. . . . Faith, hope, and love are usually transmitted by contagion from persons who possess those qualities, but the human associations which transmit them generally have transmitted also an uncritical credulity. . . . Those who are free from that uncritical credulity commonly are also free to a considerable extent from the faith, the hope, and the warm love of men which so commonly accompanied that credulity in our religious history, when nearly all men were credulous. . . . The problem of humanism is . . . to hold faithfully to a completely open-minded and critical attitude, while holding to, or eagerly seeking, the strong drives of faith, hope, and love. As such strong drives appear they will express themselves in heroic living, and by contagion will be transmitted. . . . Religion should instill a hot partisanship for life which shall set for science the task of finding significance or of creating it. 'Wishful thinking', if wisely inspired, may cause the discovery or creation of the values wished for. Our business is to find significance, or to create it.[111]

Arthur Morgan rarely talked about his personal theology, but he did on his 90th birthday when he gave a talk to his monthly meeting. He said,

> What do I mean by right conduct? It is conduct which makes me

approach the truth. What is truth? Truth is the expression of necessity . . . So, the only way I see for being free from necessity is to follow her eagerly and to hunt out her desires before she enforces them upon me. In that way she gives continually larger range to move about in. . . . I have not seen evidence which has led me to know of any order of existence beyond that of matter-energy. I do not hold that there is no such evidence, but I have seen none which impressed me, though I was desirous of being sensitive to any such. . . . With the theist, searching for the cause behind the cause, I do not wish to dispute. I only confess that the idea he holds has not been revealed to me, though I have endeavored to search honestly. . . . With weak insight, and deaf to celestial music, if any there be, I can only say in honesty I do not see angel wings or hear celestial music from other orders of being. . . . There is no easy way to an optimum course of living. . . . Objective critical study of necessity, motivated by caring much about life, and sustained by aspiration and critical imagination, gives hope of being productive. . . . I have nearly run my course. I live in the future—the future of mankind, and of life. I do not look forward to personal immortality. I see the person I call *me* as not a separate unit of life. It is a thread in the fabric of life, a moment in the course of being. Day by day I live and have my joy, as part of mankind. Day by day I live and find my joy in the future. I feel great hope, but not certainty, for human life. The issue I would live by is this: Will the continuity of life have more value because I have lived? Bodily pleasures and personal ambitions are but incidental in comparison. What sets limits of prospect for fulfillment of great hope? It probably is, I believe, the degree of caring enough about life and the will to make the utmost contribution. What do I believe for my friends and fellow men? It is that they may share to the full this great hope. I wish it because I know of no greater wish for them.[112]

Morris Mitchell (1895–1976) was the founder of Macedonia Cooperative Community, director of Putney Graduate School, and founder and president of Friends World College. One person who knew him well described him to me as an atheist but, as far as I know, Mitchell did not speak of this in public. He did write in 1967,

> In our search for truth relevant to our times, we can, and doubtless will, continue to use traditional value words, but every word must assume revised meaning. For example, among Christians the "divinity of Christ," at first threatened by the growth of objective understanding, loses its uniqueness and its superstitious qualities and becomes in a superlative degree that gift for sympathetic love with which every human is endowed. Again, to listen for the "voice of God" is to open one's being, heart, and mind in earnest, 'reverent' search for the meaning of the unfolding of the powers of truth. And a localized, personalized god becomes those all-pervasive forces and motives that govern every electron of every galaxy. . . . While Quakerism was Christian in origin, increasing numbers of Friends are humanist and hold a cosmic theology.[113]

In 1971 Bart Sobel wrote in a dissertation on Morris Mitchell,

> Mitchell is opposed to the role and practice of traditional religious institutions in society. He believes that worshipping a supreme being lessens the importance of every individual; people give up a part of themselves to an external power. . . . Mitchell believes that individuals must assume responsibility for their own actions and welfare. He wants people to rid themselves of unquestioned obedience to a supernatural authority. . . . He believes that "there is that of God in every one of us." Therefore, he feels that people must speak of the divinity of every man, woman, and child, so that they come to respect one another for the infinite capacities which they possess. . . . Mitchell sees World Education as one vehicle which will help bring about the change of emphasis from traditional religious practices to humanism. . . . In an unconventional and unorthodox way, Mitchell is a deeply religious man. . . . Mitchell

90

has devoted his life to the principles in the philosophy of World Education. . . . To Mitchell, the philosophy of World Education is not only an educational theory, not only a philosophy of life, not only a vehicle to change culture, but also a philosophy of religion.[114]

Two Quaker professors wrote about religion and philosophy from a rationalist perspective. **E. A. Burtt** (1892–1989), at Cornell University, said in a talk on Quakerism, "The Quaker concept of truth rejects the idea that there is a truth to which we should all conform. What each individual finds as he sincerely seeks for truth is the truth for him."[115] Ned Burtt was one of the signers of the Humanist Manifesto in 1933. **Richard S. Peters** (1919–2011) of London University studied the philosophy of education. He described part of the task of educators as helping us live meaningfully in a universe without inherent meaning. In 1972 he gave the Swarthmore Lecture, *Reason, Morality and Religion*.[116]

Alice and Staughton Lynd are long time advocates for peace and human rights; Alice has been draft counselor, teacher, and director of day care and health centers and Staughton has been an historian, teacher, labor lawyer, community organizer, director of freedom schools in Mississippi in 1964, and chairman of a march on Washington in 1965. Staughton rarely spoke of his nontheism but he did describe himself as an "agnostic or atheist" in an interview.[117]

In 1996 the Lynds published *Liberation Theology for Quakers*. The first paragraph is a fine declaration of faith from a humanist perspective:

> We are Quakers. We have faith that there is a potential for good in every person, and that this "inner light" needs no mediation by priest or church. We believe in treating people as equals. We believe in nonviolence and forgiveness. We disavow retaliation or retribution. We try to practice direct speaking, speaking truth to power, and living consistently with our values. We follow a simple

way of life and try to be responsible stewards of the earth and its resources. We think these are Quaker beliefs.[118]

In the same pamphlet they called for an emphasis on lives rather than doctrine:

> We believe that there is Scriptural authority for an approach to Jesus's teaching based on what people *do*, not on what they *think*. Jesus says that people who feed the hungry, visit the imprisoned, and comfort the afflicted, will experience salvation even if during their lives they are unaware of Jesus and give no thought to him (Matthew 25:31–46). Saying "Lord, Lord" is not the path to salvation, for the righteous will be known by their fruits not by their words (Matthew 7:20–21). The unbeliever who does good deeds—the Good Samaritan—will be preferred to the church member who passes by on the other side (Luke 10:30–37).[119]

Nontheist Friends

The first public expression of nontheism among Friends that I know of was the **Humanistic Society of Friends**, founded in Los Angeles in 1939. Many of the members had been Quakers, including their leader, **Lowell H. Coate** (1889–1973), but their literature did not mention Quakers. Coate later served as editor of *The Humanist World, American Rationalist,* and *The Rationalist*. The Society published *The Humanist Friend,* from 1939 to 1943, and continued as an organization until it became a chapter of the American Humanist Association in 1987. Three years later the chapter became a division of AHA. It was given responsibility for ministerial and religious humanism programs.

In 1963 **Claire Walker** wrote in *Friends Journal*, "Questing Quakers cannot feel comfortable with the supernatural in any form, but they are very clear about the crucial importance in our lives of values and implementation of values in our day-to-day living." This was followed by Joseph Havens's call for the study of post-Christian

Quakerism, and Lawrence Miller's review of John Robinson's *Honest to God* which asked what sort of God, if any, is required in religion. Later in 1964, the words "nontheist" and "nontheistic" appeared in four *Friends Journal* letters about **Daniel A. Seeger**'s successful effort to end the government practice of defining religion in terms of belief in a Supreme Being when considering applications for religious exemption from military service. Quakerism in the absence of God was now being considered.[120]

The first public gathering of nontheist Friends that I know of was the "Workshop for Non-Theistic Friends" at the FGC Gathering in Ithaca NY in 1976. Their published report was written collectively by 15 to 20 Friends led by **Robert Morgan** (1913–1992). It is a stirring declaration:

> There are non-theistic Friends. There are Friends who might be called agnostics, atheists, skeptics but who would, nevertheless, describe themselves as reverent seekers. The fifteen to twenty of us who joined this workshop did so out of the need to share ideas with others who are searching for an authentic personal religious framework. The lack of an adequate religious vocabulary which could be used as an alternative to traditional concepts has led to mistaken assumptions about individual non-traditional beliefs, thus hindering dialogue and real communication among Friends. . . . We began the workshop by sharing our struggles with words, concepts, and beliefs. We felt immediate relief that we could air our a-typical religious ideas and our fears about disclosing these in our Meetings. . . . Through discussion in pairs, in small groups and in the workshop as a whole, we became a support group, giving each other credibility, courage and stimulation. . . . In imaginative ways, all shared an eagerness to explore beyond traditional religious and Christian concepts for creative answers to life's mysteries. We share a respect and concern for all human beings. We shared an admiration for the history of Quaker altruism and, a desire to be part of our own Meeting "families." Welcoming diversity, we were

stimulated in our own thinking by listening to the beliefs of others. It is exciting to share these beliefs, but it is even more exciting to sense that we all had experienced important values and feelings that can not be adequately expressed intellectually. For us these values have given truth and meaning and zest to everyday life and an experience of religion as a growing, evolving concept. . . . Why do we belong to the Religious Society of Friends? In part because we feel the need to seek from within a loving and traditionally tolerant, gathered community. We found in our group that we were representative of a rainbow of beliefs which exists within the larger Society of Friends. This spectrum included theists who define God as a spirit or presence which intervenes and guides in a personal way. Most were non-theists who, while believing in something universal beyond our biological selves which exists in everyone, do not believe in an external directing spirit. There were seekers and questioners looking for new definitions of God free of human characteristics or not wanting to use the term God at all. Some of us explored life-energy as an evolutionary process existing in all of us and giving meaning to life. Some of us identified ourselves simply as "non-believers". . . . Recognizing that there are energies and ideas that may well be part of a new spiritual consciousness in the making, we want to develop an awareness of our diversity and a respect for it through responsibly shared dialogue. We hope for sensitivity and trust in our Meetings which allow us to grow in a community of seekers despite our differences. Unable to accept traditional theology, we are skeptical about substituting new concepts lest they become yet another theological system, but we felt it important to share the thoughts that sprang from this workshop with old and new Friends, young Friends and those who are considering becoming Friends. We believe Quakerism can accommodate this minority, and find part of its vital creativity in the process.[121]

John Linton (c.1911–2010) was one of the founders of the Quaker Universalist Group in 1977. He wrote,

This new group would be committed to the view that, however great one's reverence for the teachings and personality of Jesus, no faith can claim to be a unique revelation or to have a monopoly of truth. Because Christianity traditionally makes this claim, members of the group feel that they cannot limit themselves by calling themselves Christians. In their search for truth, and also in the interests of world peace and brotherhood, they are opposed to all divisive religious claims. They take the view that truth can be reached by more than one path. Yet because they believe in the Quaker way of life, and that Quakerism is universally valid and not dependent on Christianity, they have no wish to cut themselves off from the Society of Friends.[122]

In 1979 he wrote,

It seems to me that the Society would be greatly strengthened by the influx of people who claim to be agnostic rather than Christian and yet who sincerely share the fundamental aspirations of Quakers. I shall therefore argue not merely that the Society should admit such people as a fringe element of 'second-class members' (which is what they feel at the present), but that it should widen its own basis and give up its claim to be a specifically Christian organization. I think this should be done not just as a matter of expediency, but in the pursuit of Truth, because I believe the Truth is wider than Christianity. And I like to think that Quakerism is about the search for Truth.[123]

Kingdon W. Swayne (1920–2009) published "Confession of a Post-Christian Agnostic" in 1980. Four years later, Philadelphia Yearly Meeting selected him as their clerk. He wrote,

My own religious life can perhaps be best understood as an effort to build moral stability and connectedness by creating a web of motivation and behavior that is internally consistent and emotionally satisfying. I describe myself as post-Christian because both my best behavior and its motivations owe much to Christian thinking, though I reject most of the traditional theology. . . . If one rejects the authority [of Jesus] and most of the Christian tradition, where does one begin to build a belief system? I think I begin with the existentialist proposition that life without meaning or purpose is intolerable. Therefore one must define the meaning and purpose of one's own life. I believe this task is within my power and is my sole responsibility. I prefer to see myself not as finding and doing God's will but as striving for goodness on the basis of general principles that are derived from my own sense of the nature of the universe. . . . If I had presented this paper to Worship and Ministry of Newtown Meeting 150 years ago, would this meeting still be in session, or would I have long since been sent home in disgrace; branded a heretic? Can Worship and Ministry accept me in 1979? If you can, is this a confession of laxness on your part? Has the Religious Society of Friends lost any semblance of a core set of beliefs? Are we really comfortable with the notion that a sincere seeker may arrive at some bizarre interim conclusions on his or her road to true enlightenment, or that she or he may in fact never find the right road at all? Well I hope we are, because I would really like to stick around to see whether one day my enlightenment will come more to resemble that of George Fox or John Woolman. I would also like to stick around because the Quaker ambience does have meaning for me. . . . I grew up in the Religious Society of Friends, and I feel comfortable with many aspects of it. I like its rebellion against orthodoxy, its commitments to service and non-violence, its disdain of "hireling ministers," its careful rationality, and above all its de-ritualized ritual. . . . Writing this paper has been a richly rewarding experience. I have been forced to firm up and pull together a lot of ideas that have been floating disconnectedly through my mind. Now that I put it all together, the structure seems quite formidable. . . . I am very much alive to the possibility that some new truth may come my way that will cause the whole structure to collapse. Then what fun it will be to build a new one![124]

In 1986 Swayne wrote,

> I am a lifelong Friend who was been encouraged by his Quaker (dare I say Hicksite?) upbringing to construct his own edifice of religious meaning. My edifice is non-theistic . . . I don't think it is terribly important how Universalistic or how Christocentric the early Friends were. The important point is that late 20th century Quakerism be true to its non-creedal self. For its role in the larger religious society of our era surely is as home and refuge for those stubborn individualists who create their own theologies but need a community in which to pursue their spiritual journeys.[125]

In 1994, he wrote,

> I have since concluded that 'agnostic' was the wrong word, for the troika of believer-agnostic-atheist really limits the issue to whether or not God exists. The true issue, I think, is how best to think about the ability of humans to experience inner lives that seem in some sense to be metaphysical—beyond the physical, the rational, and the emotional. I now speak of my metaphysics as "nontheistic".[126]

Eric Johnson (c.1918–1994) wrote in "Why I am an Atheist," in 1991:

> For me God does not exist. God is an invention of human minds to help them deal with the inexplicable. . . . If you need God and believe in God, fine! But that doesn't cause God to exist. . . . Though I have no faith in God, I do seek: how to make the world better, even how to make me better. But I think faith is irresponsible. We must think—to use our minds and our bodies to make the world better. Faith is a kind of short-circuit that can destroy the mind or weaken it. Faith means: "without evidence or reason."[127]

Five months later he published a letter stating, "[The responses]

97

have been so profound, witty, and intelligent that I hereby tell you that I have been lovingly and powerfully and nonviolently forced to modify my state of mind: I hereby declare that I am no longer an atheist; I have become an agnostic."[128]

Surveys

Several surveys show the presence of nontheists among Friends. In Britain in 1989, 692 Quakers were asked "Do you believe in God?" and 26% answered "No" or "Not Sure". In Philadelphia in 2002, 56% of 552 Quakers indicated "No" or "No Definite Belief" in response to the statement, "I believe in a God to whom one can pray in the expectation of receiving an answer. *By 'answer' I mean more than the subjective, psychological effect of prayer.* [italics in the original]" In the same survey, 44% disagreed, or neither agreed nor disagreed, with the statement "I very much want a deeper spiritual relationship with God," and 52% did not agree with the statement "I have had a transcendent experience where I felt myself in the presence of God." These polls are described in David Rush's chapter in *Godless for God's Sake: Nontheism in Contemporary Quakerism*. Also see Rush's interviews with 199 nontheist Friends.[129]

Workshops

There was a nontheist workshop at the Friends General Conference Gathering in 1976, and then none until Robin Alpern, Bowen Alpern, and Glenn Mallison held one in 1996. Since then there have been one or two nontheist workshops almost every year. Robin Alpern and David Boulton have written histories of these events.[130]

In 2004 and 2011–14 there were workshops at the Woodbrooke Quaker Study Centre in Birmingham, England, and in 2005 at Pendle Hill, a Quaker center for study and contemplation near Philadelphia. These were attended by about 30 people each time. A strong desire was expressed to support other Friends, whatever their religious views are, and to be supported in turn.

There have also been nontheist Friends events at Powell House in New York Yearly Meeting, Ben Lomond Quaker Center in Pacific Yearly Meeting, and in other locations.

Internet Sites

A website with Quaker nontheist writings, blog, and email discussion group is http://www.nontheistfriends.org. It was established in 2003 and is recognized as an affinity group by Friends General Conference. Here is their welcome statement:

> Nontheistfriends.org presents the work of Friends (Quakers) who are more concerned with the natural than the supernatural. Some of us understand "God" as a symbol of human values and some of us avoid the concept while accepting it as significant to others. We differ greatly in our religious experience and in the meaning we give religious terms.
>
> We are not a pressure group trying to move Quakerism toward nontheism. We bless what our theist brothers and sisters bring to Quaker meetings and worship. All Friends have much to learn from each other. We hope to strengthen the Quaker tradition of welcoming people of diverse religious experience and to show by example that this can include nontheists.
>
> We are part of meeting communities that include theists and nontheists. Together we worship and love and cooperate, even as we differ on the particulars of our religious experience. Quakerism has been changing ever since George Fox had his first opening on Pendle Hill, becoming deeper and richer. We are all part of this living faith.
>
> On this website we seek to explore our own perspectives and to reflect on the meaning and implications of nontheism in the context of Quakerism. This is also a place where theist Friends may come to understand us better and to join in a deeper conversation. Please submit writings for posting. We also hope you will use the "comments" link at the end of each article to express your views.[131]

The Nontheist Friends Network was organized in 2011 and is a listed informal group of Britain Yearly Meeting. They have a website, http://www.nontheist-quakers.org-uk, an email discussion group and newsletter, and they sponsor an annual conference and other events. Their purposes are to:

(i) provide a supportive framework for Friends with an agnostic, humanist, atheist or related world-view, and those who experience religion as a wholly human creation;

(ii) join with all Friends who are interested in exploring varieties of nontheism as a recognised strand within modern diverse liberal Quakerism; and

(iii) strengthen and celebrate theological and spiritual diversity by promoting dialogue at all levels within the Religious Society of Friends.[132]

A leaflet of the Nontheist Friends Network contains this message:

Whether we describe ourselves as humanists, agnostics or atheists, and whether we understand God as the symbol and imagined embodiment of our highest human values or avoid the word altogether, nontheist Friends know that we don't know it all. Our various ways of being nontheist are simply various ways of being Quaker, and we celebrate the radical diversity of Quakerism, nontheist and theist. We do not see ourselves as on the Quaker fringe but as part of the broad mainstream, with something to give and much to learn from the ongoing Quaker tradition. We too are Friends and seekers.[133]

Writings

Many Quaker humanists and nontheists have published their writings, especially in recent years (see list in the Appendix, p. 135, below).

In 2006 David Boulton edited and published a collection of essays by 27 Quaker nontheists titled *Godless for God's Sake: Nontheism in Contemporary Quakerism*.[134]

This book was reviewed by Chuck Fager. He wrote,

> What have we come to in Friends religious thought, when the most exciting book of Quaker theology I've read in years is produced by a bunch of Quaker non-theists—twenty-seven in all? Well, there will be no hand-wringing about that here: I'll take thoughtful, articulate, and challenging religious thought wherever I can find it—and there's plenty of that in this compact volume. . . . What was it that The Man said? "By their fruits ye shall know them." If that's so, then as a group, nontheist Friends have as much claim to a legitimate place in contemporary Quakerism as many who feel they are defending the last true redoubt against the invading forces of unbelief. The proper response to the testimonies in these pages is not scorn or witchhunts, but an invitation to further conversation. And in my case, gratitude that these nontheists have taken the theology they don't accept seriously enough to think and write about it as thoughtfully and engagingly as they have here.[135]

Conclusion

There have always been nontheist Friends, although they have not always spoken out. There have also been Friends whose views were compatible with nontheism, such as the view that Jesus was human like the rest of us, or that the Inner Light can be identified with natural processes such as the human conscience.

In 1913 a group of adult young Friends spent a year studying the condition of the two Philadelphia Yearly Meetings. In their report they wrote,

> [O]ne of the inherited features of Hicksite Quakerism is a deliberate indifference to uniformity of belief. As the *Intelligencer* says:

"Our attitude has been one that in no way tended to uniformity of belief, and as a matter of fact we have had wide divergence of belief. We have hardly a meeting that has not had at times, at least, among its most active and influential members, those of varying shades of belief, all the way from literal interpretation of Scripture to Unitarian, agnostic and even atheistic doctrine." Most Hicksites have little interest in theology.[136]

The young Friend who wrote the report is not named but is said to have been Henry Cadbury.[137]

Since then nontheism has gradually emerged into public view. Survey data support the sense that there are nontheists in Quaker meetings today, and probably more than are generally known. Many of them may be silent for positive reasons, being comfortable in their meetings and having more important things to talk about.

Diversity is a good thing if we don't pay the price of keeping silent about what we hold dear. We are just beginning to learn how to be diverse.

One hundred years after the young Friends in Philadelphia studied how their yearly meetings might reunite, a committee of Quaker Earthcare Witness approved a statement on unity with diversity. They wrote,

> As both Friends and environmentalists we on the Spiritual Nurturance Committee of Quaker Earthcare Witness hold a variety of personal views, beliefs and approaches based in the variety of our backgrounds, traditions and experiences. We see it as good for QEW to endeavor to work with all who share our basic goals, both QEW participants and others. . . .
>
> Within the Spiritual Nurturance Committee we have collectively lived out the experience of acknowledging diversity while seeking and remaining in unity. We value inclusivity in our relations with each other. We commit ourselves to trying to focus on the spirit rather than the letter, listening and speaking from the heart, and

seeking and sharing from the heart, in the manner of Friends. We recommend this model to QEW for our work with one another and with other organizations. We offer the seeming paradox of diversity within the supportive and inclusive structure of our unity.[138]

It is good to work for acceptance of diverse philosophical points of view among Friends, especially views not held by the person speaking. Practices that facilitate the inclusion of one set of people, such as nontheists, are practices that are good for the meeting as a whole.

On these pages you have read about an incredible community of religious thinkers. It has been a joy for me to bring you together with them.

A note about
Religious Naturalism in the Time of Fox

Years ago I was struck by the phrase "All things come by nature" in George Fox's journal. These few words seemed to catch the essence of my personal philosophy. It sounded like a catch phrase that might have been used by many. A quick search of the internet found the words in confessions extracted from members of the Family of Love, a group very much like the early Friends. I asked David Boulton about it and he sent me a song the Ranters used to sing that included the phrase.

Since childhood I have enjoyed visiting other times and places, even if only through writings. I went looking for anyone in the time of Fox who might have asserted that all things come by nature. The following essay is an overview of what I found.

It is important to note that I am not trying to draw conclusions about the views of people in the time of Fox. This is not that sort of historical research. My purpose is to use the old writings to encourage people today to seek a harmonious union of religion and nature.

A final expression of gratitude, as we near the end of this book, is for the personal friends who sustained me as I sought my way through life. This family of love includes Wetherill Winder, John Bovey, Margie Frame, Reid Bush, and many, many more.

I love you all.

Religious Naturalism in the Time of Fox

As Quakerism dawned in the second half of the 1600s, religion and nature collided, and sometimes merged. Ancient Greek and Roman traditions reappeared and medieval ways long suppressed found new life. A naturalistic reformation took place in religion and science. As Rufus Jones described it,

> There was . . . a strong wave of pantheistical sentiment abroad, both on the Continent and in England. . . . The widespread pantheistic-mystical sects of the fourteenth century were never exterminated; they were rather driven down out of sight and became a submerged stream of influence. There were pretty plain upwellings of this stream during the Reformation period in Europe in the sixteenth century, and . . . it revived in England a century later.[139]

These spiritual rebels sensed that we are one with all around us and God is here, rather than in a distant heaven. The world around us is not evil; it is as good as we make it. We can be Friends with the all encompassing All.[140]

Today, again, Friends seek unity in science, religion and nature. Daniel Seeger reflected on this in an article on atheism today:

> Both science and religion rest ultimately on our contemplation of the natural world. . . . To survey any beautiful scene without distraction is to become aware of an incredible creative process that has raised all things up from the formless dust, that infuses everything with vitality and energy, that maintains balance and

lawfulness, and that illuminates each order of living things with a degree of wisdom suitable to its estate. We become aware that human existence is a part of this great web, we are humbled, and we ask what response is called for from us so that we might play our role properly in this great unfolding drama. Some religionists disparage what they call nature mysticism as a counterfeit spirituality. In truth, it is not a counterfeit spirituality but the foundation, the essence, and the core of the religious sensibility.[141]

I was drawn to this because I have been a nature lover and a Quaker as long as I can remember, and bringing them into harmony has been a central theme of my life. This took on new focus when I read in George Fox's journal, "I met with some people who had such a notion that there was no God but that all things came by nature."[142] Who would have said that to Fox, and what were their circumstances? This led to a sojourn at Pendle Hill Quaker Study Center, and a trip to the area in England where Fox's encounter happened. Then there were many visits to the Quaker libraries at Haverford and Swarthmore Colleges, hours on the internet, and hours writing.

The following review has sections on seven themes of religious naturalism: that God is in nature; that all things come by nature; our unity with creation; reaching God through nature; natural metaphors in religion; the emphasis on lives rather than notions; and relations of religion and science. You will read the words of Quakers, Seekers, Diggers, Ranters, Muggletonians, Spinozists, scientists, atheists, Boehmenites, Hermeticists, Epicureans, and Stoics. It is a vibrant community of naturalistic mystics who participated in an intellectual reformation that is still going on today.

"Creation is God himself"

Quaker Jacob Bauthumley (pronounced Bottomley) wrote in 1650, "I see that God is in all Creatures, Man and Beast, Fish and Fowle, and every green thing, from the highest Cedar to the Ivey on the wall; and that God is the life and being of them all, and that God doth really dwell, and if you will personally; if he may admit so low an expression in them all, and hath his Being no where else out of the Creatures." Bauthumley was severely punished for his vision of the unity of God, humankind, and the rest of creation. George Fox visited him in jail in 1650 and, in return, Bauthumley visited Fox in jail in 1655. Later in life Bauthumley was described as a Quaker librarian in Leicester.[143]

Quaker Gerrard Winstanley repeatedly wrote about God in nature: "The whole Creation of fire, water, Earth and Aire; and all the varieties of bodies made up thereof, is the cloathing of God: so that all things, that is A substantiall being, looked upon in the lump, is the fulnesse of him, that fills all with himself, he is in all things, and by him all things consist." He wrote, "To know the secrets of nature is to know the works of God; and to know the works of God within the creation is to know God himself, for God dwells in every visible work or body." He also wrote of "the Law of Nature (or God) as he hath written his name in every body".[144] Winstanley was a leader of the Diggers, a communal group that farmed public land and sought to radically restructure society. Once a Seeker and later a Quaker, he published 20 pamphlets between 1648 and 1652. He equated God with the law of the universe known by observation and reason guided by conscience and love. Revolutionary in religion and politics, the Diggers were suppressed. Many of their views came to be shared by early Friends, although there they were combined with more orthodox religion and politics. It is unclear what influence these writings had on Friends, but they show us something of the cultural environment in which Quakerism developed.[145]

John Everard, a leader of the Seekers and an inspiration for Friends, wrote, "The whole creation is God's house, God's temple, but we see it not so; we see not God in all places, nor in all creatures, . . . till our eyes be opened. God is always in every creature and he is there alike, in his Heaven, and in his Holy place, and he cannot be more in one then another"[146] William Penn described Everard as "that renowned Independent," "that great spiritual separatist," and "that notable and very religious man."[147] Rufus Jones wrote of Everard, "He is, I feel sure, the father of the [Seeker] movement. More than any other man in England Everard absorbed the central teaching of the Continental spiritual reformers, appropriated these principles and made them his own through personal experience, became himself a dynamic spiritual organ, and, set aflame with burning light and truth, made a host of converts."[148]

Richard Coppin, a Seeker, wrote in 1649, "God is all in one, and so is in everyone. The same all which is in me, is in thee; the same God which dwells in one dwells in another, even in all; and in the same fullness as he is in one, he is in everyone." William Penn listed Coppin's works among "Books forrunning Friends appearance".[149]

An anonymous Ranter wrote, "[E]very creature in the first estate of creation was God, and every creature is God, every creature that hath life and breath being an efflux from God, and shall return into God again, be swallowed up in him as a drop in the ocean." Another Ranter is reported to have said, "If God be all things, . . . then he is this Dog, this Tobacco-pipe, he is me and I am him".[150]

Before there were Quakers, Jacob Boehme wrote, "[C]onsider how the *whole Nature,* with . . . the Extention, Depth, and Heighth [of] Heaven and Earth . . . is together the *Body* or Corporeity of God; and the Powers of the Stars are the Fountain Veins in the natural Body of God, *in this World.*" He also wrote, "In this light my spirit suddenly saw through all, and in and by all, the creatures; even in herbs and grass it knew God". Again, he wrote, "We can, therefore, in no wise say that God's essence is something far off, which possesses a special abode or place; for the abyss of Nature and creation is God himself."[151] During the 1640s the writings of Jacob Boehme became available in English. It was the time of Oliver Cromwell and the Commonwealth of England and there was new liberty to speak and publish openly, and people did. Jacob Boehm's nature mysticism was embraced by many of the nonconforming sects, including Friends.[152]

Baruch Spinoza in Holland also united God and nature. In a letter in 1662 he wrote, "I could not separate God from Nature, as all of whom I have any knowledge have done." In his *Ethics* he mentioned "God, or Nature" four times; here is an example: "Nature does not act with an end in view; that eternal and infinite being we call God, or Nature, acts from the same necessity from which he exists." It is said that Spinoza knew Quakers in Amsterdam and translated one of Margaret Fell's pamphlets from English to Hebrew. His friend and colleague, Peter Balling, wrote *Light on the Candlestick* in 1662 which represented Friends views so well that they adopted it as their own. On July 24, 1678, the scientist Robert Hooke wrote in his diary, "Much discourse about Spinosa quakers."[153]

Shortly after the time of Fox, John Toland used the term "pantheist" to describe a person for whom God is nature. In 1720 he wrote, "All Things in the World are one, And one is All in all Things.....What's All in all Things is GOD, Eternal and Immense, Neither begotten, nor ever to perish." Toland cited Heraclitus as his source: "All things are from the All, and the All is from all Things."[154] (The term "panentheist" was invented in 1828 to represent someone for whom God is in nature and beyond nature.)

All this was heresy, of course. The first words of the Blasphemy Act of 1650 were directed at those who associated God with nature:

> That any persons not distempered in their brains, who shall maintain any meer creature to be God; or to be Infinite, Almighty, or in Honor, Excellency, Majesty, and Power to be equal and the same with the true God or that the true God or the Eternal Majesty dwells in the creature, or that shall deny the holiness of God ... shall suffer six months' imprisonment for the first offence; and for the second shall be banished; and if they return without licence shall be treated as felons.[155]

Fox rejected the full association of God and nature, carefully distinguishing between humans and the rest of nature. This came up when people asked him whether the Light within is natural. This happened repeatedly in England, Wales and Scotland.[156] Here is a notable example:

> [W]e were moved to speak to Oliver Cromwell concerning the sufferings of Friends and laid before him and directed him to the light of Christ who had enlightened every man that cometh into the world: and he said it was a natural light, and we showed him the contrary, and how it was divine and spiritual from Christ the spiritual and heavenly man, which was called the life in Christ, the Word and the light in us.[157]

"All things come by nature"

What are the limits of nature mysticism? If God becomes nature, is God naturalized or nature spiritualized? George Fox faced these questions as he was beginning his ministry. He was 24 years old in 1648, in the Vale of Belvoir (pronounced Beaver), a broad valley with low hills at the sides, just east of Nottingham. As he wrote in his journal,

> And one morning, as I was sitting by the fire, a great cloud came over me, and a temptation beset me; but I sat still. And it was said, "All things come by nature;" and the elements and stars came over me so that I was in a manner quite clouded with it. But inasmuch as I sat, still and silent, the people in the house perceived nothing. And as I sat still under it and let it alone, a living hope arose in me, and a true voice, which said, "There is a living God who made all things." And immediately the cloud and temptation vanished away, and life rose over it all, and my heart was glad, and I praised the living God. And after some time, I met with some people who had such a notion that there was no God but that all things came by nature. And I had great dispute with them and overturned them and made some of them confess that there was a living God. Then I

110

saw that it was good that I had gone through that exercise. And we had great meetings in those parts, for the power of the Lord broke through in that side of the country.[158]

The incident has been reprinted in Friends publications many times and was the basis of John Greenleaf Whittier's poem, "Revelation."[159]

Wondering who used the phrase "All things come by nature" in Fox's time, I soon found that Lodowicke Muggleton described an experience in his own journal that is very much like the incident in the Vale. (The similarity was noted by William C. Braithwaite.[160]) It included this line: "Many of my Acquaintance did say in their Hearts, and Tongues both, *That there is no God, but nature only.*" He also wrote in 1662, "For this I do affirm by that spirit of faith which is in me, that if God be not a person or form, a spiritual body in the form of a man, then I say that there is not God at all, but nature only."[161]

Fox and Muggleton started religious movements at about the same time and on one occasion had a public debate that didn't go well for Fox. Later, Friends and Muggletonians carried on a pamphlet war.

There is also a version of this story in the writings of Jacob Boehme. Like Fox and Muggleton, Boehme contemplated nature and was depressed by it: "I fell into a very deep and melancholy and heavy sadness, when I beheld and contemplated the great Deep of this world, also the sun and stars, the clouds, rain and snow, and considered in my spirit the whole creation of the world." Fox and Muggleton turned to a creator God, but Boehme's solution was to find God in all creation: "In this light my spirit suddenly saw through all, and in and by all, the creatures; even in herbs and grass it knew God, who he is and how he is and what his will is. And suddenly in that light my will was set on by a mighty impulse to describe the Being of God."[162]

The phrase is similar to one in a Ranters' carol of 1650: "They prate of God, believe it Fellow Creature, / There's no such Bugbear,

111

all was made by nature". The Ranters were known to hold boisterous meetings in taverns and sing songs set to the tune of church hymns.[163]

The phrase also appears in forced confessions, although in these sad circumstances we don't know who suggested it.[164]

The person who uttered the words to Fox might have been an atheist. In the seventeenth century a person could be called an atheist for many views, for instance holding that Jesus is only a man, or the soul is mortal. An atheist might not deny God but simply fail to assert that there is a God. The popularity of atheism is suggested by the passionate literature published against it at this time, some of it by leading scholars. Two examples are William Charleton's *The Darkness of Atheism Dispelled by the Light of Nature* (1652), and Henry More's *An Antidote to Atheism* (dedicated to Quaker Anne Conway in 1653).

Most atheists kept quiet, but a few repeatedly expressed their views in public over a period of years. They were apparently protected by powerful friends. An interesting example is Huntingdon Plumptre (d. 1660), a physician and member of the Nottingham city government. He was highly argumentative, even challenging his friends to duels. On one occasion he was tried for heresy but acquitted. Here is a description of the man: "Plumptre was a doctor of physic, an inhabitant of Nottingham, who had learning, natural parts, and understanding enough to discern between natural civil righteousness and injustice; but he was a horrible atheist, and had such an intolerable pride that he brooked no superiors, and having some wit, took the boldness to exercise it in the abuse of all gentlemen wherever he came."[165]

This was written by Lucy Hutchinson, the wife of John Hutchinson, the Governor of Nottingham who protected George Fox when he was arrested in 1649. The Hutchinsons were Baptists and lived in Owthorpe on the eastern edge of Nottingham, between the city and the Vale of Belvoir further east. The doctor was a sometime friend of the Hutchinsons and he was their physician; she even painted his portrait.[166] (This is not the family of Anne Marbury Hutchinson, the New England Puritan, whose husband's family was from Lincoln.)

Searching further back in time, we find Jacob Boehme using a similar phrase in 1612: "Reason says: . . . all things happen by chance; there is no God who interests himself in the sufferer . . . Answer . . . there must be a God who has brought it into a life and will."[167] Boehme seems to have patterned this after Thomas Aquinas who wrote in 1274, "Objection 2. . . . But it seems that everything we see in the world can be accounted for by other principles, supposing God did not exist. . . . Reply to Objection 2. Since nature works for a determinate end under the direction of a higher agent, whatever is done by nature must needs be traced back to God, as to its first cause."[168]

The phrase also resembles a passage in *The Divine Pymander* by Hermes Trismegistus, compiled before 200, a book Boehme cited as one of his sources of inspiration: "Now this wight [creature] if it shall come to learn or know, that the world was once made, and all things are done according to Providence and Necessity, Destiny, or Fate, bearing Rule over all; Will he not be much worse than himself, despising the whole because it was made." This is followed by a description of an experience by a youth talking with God about nature that has some of the features of the stories by Fox, Muggleton, and Boehme. *The Divine Pymander* was translated by John Everard and published in English in 1649, the year after the incident in the Vale incident, although manuscripts were already in circulation.[169]

In about 175 Marcus Aurelius, the Stoic philosopher and emperor, wrote, "All that is harmony for thee, O Universe, is in harmony with me as well. Nothing that comes at the right time for thee is too early or too late for me. Everything is fruit to me that thy seasons bring, O Nature. All things come of thee, have their being in thee, and return to thee." This was published in English in 1634. The similarity of Quakerism and Stoicism was noticed by William Penn who urged a Friend to include Seneca, Marcus Aurelius and Epictetus in his library.[170]

113

The phrase we have been following echoes a line in the poem *On the Nature of Things (De Rerum Natura)*, by Titus Lucretius Carus:

Meantime, when once we know from nothing still
Nothing can be create, we shall divine
More clearly what we seek: those elements
From which alone all things created are,
And how accomplished by no tool of Gods.[171]

Lucretius was a Roman who described the materialist philosophy of Epicurus (341–270BCE) in easily read verse in about 50BCE. A copy was found in 1417 and first published in 1473. Many editions followed and Lucretius's work influenced philosophers, scientists, and artists.

Surprisingly, close to the time of Fox's experience in the Vale and only a few miles away, Lucy Hutchinson, the friend of Dr. Plumptre, was writing an English version of Lucretius's Latin poem. As her son later described it,

She had heard the doctrines of Epicurus and the atomic theory talked of, and out of curiosity and the desire to instruct herself read and translated the six books of the *De Rerum Natura*. "I turned it into English in a room where my children practiced the several qualities they were taught with their tutors, and I numbered the syllables of my translation by the threads of the canvas I wrought in, and set them down with a pen and ink that stood by me."[172]

This is thought to have been between 1645 and 1655. Lucretius's poem was well known in Latin but was not available in English until a small portion was published in 1656, and the entire poem in 1682.[173]

"Unity with the creation"

George Fox had a strong sense of unity with God's creation but he did not mean that God was in creation, aside from human beings. This was a subtle but important distinction.

Fox wrote in his journal:

> The creation was opened to me; and it was showed me how all things had their names given them according to their nature and virtue. . . . Great things did the Lord lead me into, and wonderful depths were opened unto me, beyond what can by words be declared; but as people come into subjection to the Spirit of God, and grow up in the image and power of the Almighty, they may receive the Word of wisdom that opens all things, and come to know the hidden unity in the Eternal Being.[174]

This is similar to a passage in Boehme's writings and has been offered as evidence of the influence of Boehme among early Friends.[175]

For Fox, nature was created for the benefit of humankind and the glory of God:

> For the Lord showed me, that . . . I was to keep to 'yea' and 'nay' in all things; . . . using the creatures in their service, as servants in their places, to the glory of Him that created them; they being in their covenant, and I being brought up into the covenant, as sanctified by the Word which was in the beginning, by which all things are upheld; wherein is unity with the creation.[176]

A commitment to unity with nature can be combined with a variety of philosophies and a variety of environmental ethics.

On one occasion in 1652 Fox was particularly concerned to demonstrate unity with creation. As he later wrote in his journal,

> [T]here came John Story to me, and lighted his pipe of tobacco,

and, said he, "Will you take a pipe of tobacco," saying, "Come, all is ours"; and I looked upon him to be a forward, bold lad. Tobacco I did not take, but it came into my mind that the lad might think I had not unity with the creation, for I saw he had a flashy, empty notion of religion; so I took his pipe and put it to my mouth and gave it to him again to stop him lest his rude tongue should say I had not unity with the creation.[177]

This may relate to the Ranter saying about God in a tobacco pipe, quoted above.

The Stoics emphasized the unity of nature. Early Friends may have been familiar with this passage from Marcus Aurelius's *Meditations*:

Whatsoever doth happen in the world, is, in the course of nature, as usual and ordinary as a rose in the spring, and fruit in summer. Of the same nature is sickness and death; slander, and lying in wait, and whatsoever else ordinarily doth unto fools use to be occasion either of joy or sorrow. That, whatsoever it is, that comes after, doth always very naturally, and as it were familiarly, follow upon that which was before. For thou must consider the things of the world, not as a loose independent number, consisting merely of necessary events; but as a discreet connection of things orderly and harmoniously disposed.[178]

Stoicism provided a model for the collective personality of Friends with its call for calm centering before action, accepting the will of God or universe, releasing ones personal agenda, concern for daily life rather than notions about life, common sense, practical education, sobriety, patience, and kindliness.

In 1682 Penn wrote in the Preface of *Some Fruits of Solitude,* "Reader,—This Enchiridion, I present thee with, is the Fruit of Solitude: A School few care to learn in, tho' None instructs us better. Some Parts of it are the Result of serious Reflection: Others the Flashings of Lucid Intervals: Writ for private Satisfaction, and now

116

publishe'd for an Help to Human Conduct." "Enchiridion" means "handbook" in Greek and the title of the famous manual of ethical advice of Epictetus is *The Enchiridion* (published in English in 1567, 1610, 1670, 1692, and 1694).[179]

In 1871 David Duncan, one of the progressive Free Friends of Manchester, England, wrote in an essay on John Woolman:

> There was greatness about him of the true sort, a greatness un-common; he reminds us of Epictetus, of Marcus Aurelius, but we cannot find a parallel amongst the churches. . . . John Woolman was not a student or a scholar; but he was much more, a man who guided his actions, great and small, by an active intelligence which saw God's work and will visibly present, and which pressed through the narrow limits of the flesh to communion with all nature.[180]

"We show you the Deity"

It is possible to see nature as God's handiwork and as a path to God, whatever position we take on God's presence in nature. (There is support for this approach in the Bible.[181])

Jacob Boehme wrote, "(W)e show you the Manifestation of the Deity through Nature."[182] Gerrard Winstanley called on us to "dive into the secret of the Creation, that they may learn to see and know God (the Spirit of the whole Creation) in all his works".[183]

William Penn wrote of "The World wearing the *Mark* of its Maker, whose Stamp is everywhere *visible*, and the *Characters* very *legible* to the Children of Wisdom."[184]

Quaker scientist Robert Boyle saw his work as a path to God. As his biographer explained, "[S]urprising is Boyle's use of the *Pymander* of Hermes Trismegistus . . . which appears to have reinforced his almost mystical sense of the role of the study of nature in raising man's mind towards God."[185]

About 100 years later, the Quaker botanist in Pennsylvania, John Bartram, apparently felt the same way. He wrote, "My head runs all upon the works of God in nature. It is through that telescope I see God in his glory."[186]

"An ocean of light and love"

The early Friends used metaphors derived from nature. They wrote and spoke about the light and the seed; the cleansing fire and the sweet, still, flowing river; the way and the life; the mother, father, and children.

In Jacob Boehme's first book, *Aurora, or The Rising Dawn*, the first words are, "Courteous Reader, I compare the whole *Philosophy*, *Astrology*, and *Theology*, together with their mother, to a goodly tree which groweth in a fair garden of pleasure." The next eleven short paragraphs mention trees, sap, earth, branches, fruit, cold, heat, mildew, caterpillars, worms, men, stars, moisture, blossoms, apples, mould, wind, rain, tempest, stems, suckers, roots, twigs, fire, elements, flames, gardens, sun, snow, frost, poison, kernels, and nature (eight times). With these are references to Deity, God, Creator, Holy Ghost, heavenly, hellish, good, evil, and spirit. This was the religion of Jacob Boehme.[187]

The ocean provided a powerful metaphor. Fox wrote, "I saw also that there was an ocean of darkness and death, but an infinite ocean of light and love which flowed over the ocean of darkness." The Digger, Gerrard Winstanley, wrote, "[Y]ou must be dead to your customs before you can run into the sea of truth." The Seeker, Joseph Salmon, wrote, "[M]y soul spilt and emptied into the fountain and ocean of divine fullness". This metaphor continues today in the name of the humanist Sea of Faith Network.[188]

In 1653 John Everard addressed the question of our place in nature by imagining a remarkable conversation between two drops of water. The first drop asks,

"Whence are we? Canst thou conceive whence we are? Dost thou know either whence we come or to whom we belong, or whither we shall go? Something we are, but what will in a short time become of us, canst thou tell?" And the other drop might answer, "Alas poor fellow-drop, be assured we are nothing, for the sun may arise and draw us up and scatter us and so bring us to nothing." Says the other again, "Suppose it do, for all that, yet we are, we have a being, we are something." "Why, what are we?" saith the other. "Why, brother drop, dost thou not know? We, even we, as small and as contemptible as we are in ourselves, yet we are members of the Sea; poor drops though we be, yet let us not be discouraged: *We belong to the vast Ocean.*"[189]

Everard also wrote of "playing with cockel-shells and pebble-stones that lie on the outcoasts of the Kingdom." Later, John Milton called Stoic philosophers "Children gathering pebbles on the shore", and Isaac Newton wrote, "I seem to have been only like a boy, playing on the sea-shore, and diverting myself, in now and then finding a smoother pebble or prettier shell than ordinary, whilst the great ocean of truth lay all undiscovered before me."[190]

Nature provided a rich vocabulary for Friends and others in Fox's time.

"Likeness to Christ rather than notions of Christ"

Religious naturalists tend to be concerned with our behavior rather than theories explaining the behavior. A memorial for the Seeker, John Everard, states, "He would often say that he desired to be acquainted with men who had experience with Christ rather than men of notions and speculations, [men] *that desired to act rather than to talk.*" William Penn urged us to follow a similar path when he wrote, "Christians ought to be distinguished by their likeness to Christ, and not their notions of Christ". Over a century later, Lucretia Mott said, "It is time that Christians were judged more by their likeness to Christ than their notions of Christ. Were this sentiment generally admitted we should not see such tenacious adherence to what men deem the opinions and doctrines of Christ while at the same time in every day practise is exhibited anything but a likeness to Christ."[191]

Another example of Friends caution concerning words is the admonition from the Elders of Balby in 1656: "Dearly beloved Friends, these things we do not lay upon you as a rule or form to walk by, but that all with a measure of the light which is pure and holy may be guided, and so in the light walking and abiding, these things may be fulfilled in the Spirit,—not from the letter, for the letter killeth, but the Spirit giveth life."[192]

This had been a theme in the writings and sermons of John Everard. He wrote, "The Letter, the Scriptures are *all True,* as I said before: but let me tell you withal, they are true onely as God means them. We must give him leave *To interpret* his own meaning: He that wrote the Scriptures, certainly knows best *His own mind in them:* but I say, if you have *Onely* the Letter, Nay, though ye have the external signification of them, that *kills,* that *destroyes.* So in the same sense is it spoken concerning the Word: *The Letter kills, but the Spirit gives life.*"[193] (The last phrase is from II Corinthians 3:6.)

Gerrard Winstanley made the same point: "The whole Scriptures are but a report of spiritual mysteries, held forth to the eye of flesh in words, but to be seen in the substantial matter of them by the eye of the spirit." This was also in the literature of Hendrick Niclaes of the Family of Love, a century before the Quakers: "For the written word of the letter is not the word itself, that cleanseth and sanctifieth the man from the sin, or which procreateth the life, but the same is a shadow or figuring out of the holy and true word, and a serviceable instrument whereby we are made well affected, (inwardly in our souls) to the true word of Vivification".[194]

In a diverse religious community, we can interpret each other's words as we interpret Scripture, reaching from our hearts to the sources and purposes of each other's words.

It is imperative that words not be our only actions. Winstanley wrote: "God who is the King of righteousness, is not a God of words only, but of deedes; for it is the badge of hypocrisie, for a man to say, and not to do. Therefore we leave this with you all, having peace in our hearts, by declaring faithfully to you, this light that is in us, and which we do not onley speake and write, but which we do easily act & practise."[195]

As Friends, we are taught to prepare ourselves well and then trust our reactions. This approach was familiar to early Friends. John Everard wrote, "Turn the man loose who has found the living Guide within him, and then let him neglect the outward if he can; just as you would say to a man who loves his wife with all tenderness, 'you may beat her, hurt her or kill her, if you want to!'"[196]

This apparent disregard for laws is called antinomianism and it has an ancient pedigree. A member of the Brethren of the Free Spirit wrote in about 1330, "The free man is quite right to do whatever gives him pleasure." St. Augustine wrote in about 406, "Love, and do what thou wilt".[197]

Early Friends were concerned with daily life. As Henry Cadbury noted, "I think we often tend to rationalize as tho [action] all grows out of some Christian or Quaker historical attitude that can be articulated. Our predecessors did not usually do so. Their action was much more spontaneous than inquiry as to whether it fitted a belief, e.g. as in the inner light. If what they did actually did fit, I think that was a later discovery." Cadbury summarized, "I have the feeling that the purest influence has often been unplanned, the by-product of conscientious spiritual living."[198]

This approach may have been behind the story of Penn and his sword. Supposedly, when William Penn first attended Friends meetings, in about 1667, he wore a sword, as had been his custom. He asked Fox about this and Fox said, "I advise thee to wear it as long as thou canst." Penn soon stopped wearing the sword, later telling Fox, "I wore it as long as I could."[199]

Some consider the story apocryphal because it seems contrary to the peace testimony and wasn't published until 1852. To me, it sounds like Fox giving a lesson in Everard's antinomian ethics. There is an implied commitment by Fox to support Penn as he works out his dilemma. Leaving Penn's decision to Penn doesn't mean Fox would approve any outcome. There is no presumption that the individual may run wild; on the contrary, the community is involved in the individual's clearness process, balancing the excess of individual imaginative enthusiasm, that Friends knew something about.

"We cannot miss of being good Naturalists"

Scientists and Quakers share an outlook. They draw knowledge directly from experience rather than from what people say about it. Waiting and observing are key practices. The aim is practical improvement in our world, and they are generally optimistic that this is possible. Simplicity and honesty are declared values.

Science seeks to explain observations in terms of other observations, and to refrain from speculation about what may or may not be beyond this. Individual scientists often divide their repertoires, being scientific in some areas and not in others. In science as in religion, common practices unite people who differ in how they talk.

Scientist William Harvey sounded like a Friend when he wrote, "The too familiar vice of the present age is to obtrude as manifest truths, mere fancies, born of conjecture and superficial reasoning, altogether unsupported by the testimony of sense." The motto of the Royal Society of London for the Improvement of Knowledge, founded in 1660, is *Nullius in verba*, translated as *Take nobody's word for it*.[200]

Gerrard Winstanley based knowledge on sense: "All outward glory that is at a distance from the five senses . . . is of a transient nature; and so is the heaven that your preachers tell you of." (Here he reverses what theologists consider to be eternal and transitory.) The Diggers, like the Quakers, held that truth starts with experience: "What I hear another man speak is nothing to me until I find the same experience in myself; the testimony of others is known to be true by the testimony of the same experience within myself." Again,

Winstanley described the Diggers' commitment to observation: "And every one who speaks of any Herb, Plant, Art, or Nature of Mankind, is required to speak nothing by imagination, but what he hath found out by his own industry and observation in tryal . . . By this means, in time men shall attain to the practical knowledge of God truly".[201]

For Winstanley, speculation was the work of the devil:

> And if a man should go to imagine, what God is beyond the Creation, or what he will be in a spiritual demonstration after a man is dead, he doth as the proverb saith, build castles in the air, or tells us of a world beyond the Moon, and beyond the Sun, meerly to blinde the reason of man. . . . God manifests himself in actual knowledge, not in imagination; he is still in motion, either in bodies upon earth, or in the bodies in the heavens, or in both; in the night and in the day, in Winter, in Summer, in cold, in heat, in growth or not in growth.[202]

The early scientists and the early Quakers had contact with each other. In his journal, Fox proposes an experiment to compare the resistance to decay of consecrated and unconsecrated wine and bread. Thomas Lawson (1630–1691), one of the Valiant Sixty, was a schoolmaster and botanist, and tutor of Margaret Fell's children and grandchildren. Thomas Lower (1633–1720), physician and husband of Mary Fell, was Fox's stepson-in-law and the scribe and editor when Fox dictated the first draft of his journal. Lower's brother, Richard (1632–91), was an early member of the Royal Society of London. Quaker Anne Conway (1631–1678/9) wrote about philosophy from a vitalist perspective. Her family was closely related to William Harvey and the Royal Society: her father was Harvey's executor, a brother married Harvey's niece and was instrumental in getting approval of the charter for the Royal Society, and another brother was a founding member of the Royal Society and author of a book on materialist philosophy, now lost. Quaker scientist Robert Boyle sought to love God by studying nature. His brother, Roger Boyle, was a friend Anne Conway's husband, Edward, and Boyle's sister, Katherine Jones, was Anne's friend and neighbor.[203]

George Fox valued nature because of its agricultural products and medicinal herbs. He also depended on nature walks as part of his personal clearness process. William Penn, 20 years younger than Fox, had a broader view of nature. He was listed as a member of the Royal Society, perhaps because of his passion for collecting and studying the plants of Pennsylvania. In 1683 Penn wrote to a friend,

> I value my selfe much upon ye good opinion of those ingeneous Gentlemen I know of ye Royall Society, and their kind wishes for me and my poor Province: all I can say is that I and It are votarys to ye prosperity of their harmless and usefull Inquierys. It is even one step to Heaven to returne to nature, and though I love that proportion should be observed in all things, yett a naturall Knowledge, or ye Science of things from Sence and a carefull observation and argumentation thereon, reinstates men, and gives them some possession of themselves again; a thing they have long wanted by an ill tradition, too closely followed and ye foolish Credulity so Incident to men. I am a Greshamist throughout . . .[204] [The Royal Society met at Gresham College.]

In *Some Fruits of Solitude* William Penn wrote,

> The *World* is certainly a great and stately *Volume* of natural Things; and may be not improperly styled the *Hieroglyphicks* of a better: But alas! how very few Leaves of it do we seriously turn over! This ought to be the *Subject* of the Education of our *Youth* . . . It were Happy if we studied Nature more in natural Things; and acted according to Nature; whose Rules are *few, plain and most reasonable*. Let us begin where she begins, go her Pace, and close always where she ends, and we cannot miss of being good *Naturalists*.[205]

Conclusion

The seventeenth century nature mystics sought to be included in religion and in science. They failed in both. Science spurned speculation as the path to knowledge. The religion of scientists could vary and was left up to the individual. Science was not about to embrace a particular religion, even one that had nature at its heart. Science and religion divided the world into two realms, and this allowed science to survive.

Religion, in turn, had trouble moving beyond its ancient distinction between God and nature. The division into realms helped religion withstand the assault of science.

The upwelling of nature mysticism in the mid and late seventeenth century presented a challenge to Friends. They wrestled with how to unite God and nature. For many, nature represented a path to God, a God they found within each of us. A few went further and found God throughout nature.

The story of the nature mystics of Fox's time can be an inspiration for both nature loving spiritualists and Quaker loving naturalists.

Today, Friends unite religion and nature in many ways. For some God and nature are separate realms, or God may be in nature but also apart from it, or not apart from it, or just in humans, or not anywhere. Each Friend seeks an appropriate path, and does so as part of a wider Friends community.

This leads to many questions, and some answers, and more questions. And yet even as we differ, we have found unity.

Friends, we are on a nature walk together. It started with the birth of our Society. The path is broad and it is open to many varieties of Friends, to scientists and nonscientists, theists and nontheists, Christians and nonChristians, and so on.

Let us support each other on this walk. Let us join in loving each other and loving the rest of nature.

Appendix

"Nullius in verba" . . . *"Take nobody's word for it".*
—Royal Society of London for the Improvement of Knowledge (p. 122)

Appendix Contents

Glossary

From *The Oxford English Dictionary*, 2nd ed.
[Cross references to pages, above, in brackets.]

behaviour: Manner of conducting oneself in the external relations of life; demeanor, deportment. Bearing, manners. . . . The manner in which a thing acts under specified conditions or circumstances, or in relation to other things. [See p. 44, above.]

cause: That which produces an effect; that which gives rise to any action, phenomenon, or condition. . . . Cause and effect are correlative terms. [p. 43]

control: n. the fact of controlling, or the checking and directing actions; the function or powers of directing and regulating; domination, command, sway. . . . v. To exercise restraint or direction upon the free action of; to hold sway over, exercise power or authority over; to dominate, command. [p. 43]

determinism: The philosophical doctrine that human action is not free but necessarily determined by motives which are regarded as external forces acting upon the will. [p. 43]

effect: Something accomplished, caused, or produced; a result, consequence. Correlative with CAUSE. [p. 43]

environment: Objects or the region surrounding anything . . . The conditions under which any person or thing lives or is developed;

the sum-total of influences which modify and determine the development of life or character. [p. 41]

environmentalism: One who believes in or promotes the principles or precepts of environmentalism; also, one who is concerned with the preservation of the environment (from pollution, etc.).

free will: Spontaneous will, unconstrained choice (to do or act). Often in phr. Of one's own free will, and the like. . . . "The power of directing our own actions without constraint by necessity or fate." (Samuel Johnson's *Dictionary*) [p. 46]

materialism: The opinion that nothing exists except matter and its movements and modifications; also, in a more limited sense, the opinion that the phenomena of consciousness and will are wholly due to the operation of natural agencies.

natural: Constituted by nature; having a basis in the normal constitution of things . . . Of sciences, or methods of combination, arrangement, classification, etc. . . . *natural order*, the order apparent in the constitution of matter and operation of forces in nature. . . . *natural theology*, theology based upon reasoning from the natural facts apart from revelation. . . . Having a real or physical existence, as opposed to what is spiritual, intellectual, fictitious, etc. . . . Pertaining to, operating or taking place in, the physical (as opposed to the spiritual) world. . . . Existing within, or formed by, nature; consisting of objects of this kind; not artificially made, formed, or constructed. [p. 41]

naturalism: A view of the world, and of man's relation to it, in which only the operation of natural (as opposed to supernatural or spiritual) laws and forces is admitted or assumed. [p. 41]

naturalist: One who studies natural, in contrast to spiritual, things;

one who regards natural causes as a sufficient explanation of the world and its phenomena; an adherent of or believer in, naturalism. [p. 41]

nature: The natural world, or its collective objects and phenomena, esp. those with which man is most directly in contact; freq. the features and products of the earth itself, as contrasted with those of human civilization. [p. 41]

physical: Of or pertaining to material nature, or to the phenomenal universe, perceived by the senses; pertaining to or connected with matter; material; opposed to psychical, mental, spiritual. . . . Of or pertaining to Natural Philosophy or natural Science; of, pertaining or relating to, or in accord with, the regular processes or laws of nature. [p. 41]

psychology: The science of the nature, functions, and phenomena of the human mind (formerly also of the soul). . . . In mod. usage, the signification of the word has broadened to include (a) the scientific study of the mind as an entity and in its relationship to the physical body. [the following quotation is from their entry for **behaviour**] "Psychology, as the behaviorist views it, is a purely objective experimental branch of natural science. Its theoretical goal is the prediction and control of behavior. . . . (John B. Watson, *Psychol. Rev.* XX 1913 p. 158)" [p. 44]

religion: Action or conduct indicating a belief in, reverence for, and desire to please a divine ruling power; the exercise or practice of rites or observances implying this. . . . A particular system of faith and worship. . . . Recognition on the part of man of some higher unseen power as having control of his destiny and as being entitled to obedience, reverence, and worship; the general mental and moral attitudes resulting from this belief, with reference to its effects upon the individual or the community; personal or general acceptance of

133

the feeling as a standard of spiritual and practical life. . . . Devotion to some principle; strict fidelity or faithfulness; conscientiousness, pious affect or attachment. [p. 48]

science: A knowledge acquired by study; acquaintance with or mastery of any department of learning. . . . In a more restricted sense: A branch of study which is concerned either with a connected body of demonstrated truths or with observed facts systematically classified and more or less colligated by being brought under general laws, and which includes trustworthy methods for the discovery of new truths within its own domain. [p. 41]

spiritual: Of or pertaining to, affecting or concerning, the spirit or higher mental qualities, esp. as regarded in a religious aspect. (Freq. in express or implied distinction to bodily, corporal, or temporal.) [p. 48]

Publications on Quaker Nontheism

I regret missing some publications. Please send copies or references for material you would like others to know about to this address: oscresson@juno.com.

Earlier Publications (1962–1995)

Allott, Stephen. "Quaker Agnosticism." *The Friends Quarterly* 25, no. 6 (1989): 252–58.

Allott, Stephen. "Is God Objective Fact?" *The Friends Quarterly* 28, no. 4 (1994): 158–66.

Banks, John. "Simply the Thing I Am." *The Friends Quarterly* 27, no. 7 (1993): 317–22.

Barbour, Ian G. *Science and Secularity: The Ethics of Technology*. NY: Harper & Row, 1970.

Boland, James R. "An Agnostic's Apology." Poem. *Friends Journal* 15, no. 13 (July 1/15 1969): 391.

Boulding, Kenneth. "Machines, Men, and Religion." *Friends Journal* 14, no. 24 (December 15, 1968): 643–44.

Brayshaw, Maude. "The Search for God." In Friends Home Service Committee, *In Search of God: Some Quaker Essays*. London: printed by author, 1966, pp. 5–6.

Cadbury, Henry J. "A Quaker Honest to God." *Friends Journal* 10, no. 13 (July 1, 1964): 298–99.

Creasey, Maurice A. *Bearings or Friends and the New Reformation*. Swarthmore Lecture. London: Friends Home Service Committee, 1969.

Crom, Scott. "Human Experience and Religious Faith." *Friends Journal* 11, no. 17 (September 1, 1965): 429–31.

Crom, Scott. "The Trusting Agnostic." Comments by Maurice H. Friedman and John H. McCandless, and response to comments by Scott Crom. *Quaker Religious Thought* 14, no. 2 (1972): 1–39.

Crom, Scott. "Intellectual Bankruptcy and Religious Solvency (Part I)". *Friends Journal* 13, no. 21 (November 1, 1967): 566–68.

Crom, Scott. "Intellectual Bankruptcy and Religious Solvency (Part II)". *Friends Journal* 13, no. 22 (November 15, 1967): 599–600.

Evans, Cadifor. "The Appeal of Quakerism to the Agnostic." In Friends Home Service Committee, *In Search of God: Some Quaker Essays*. London: printed by author, 1966, pp. 7–13.

Fuchs, Peter. "A Quaker Wannabe—Maybe." *Friends Journal* 41, no. 5 (May 1995): 10–11.

Friends Journal. "The New Atheism" and "The Turning Point." Editorials. *Friends Journal* 8, no. 12 (June 15, 1962): 251.

Havens, Joseph. "Christian Roots and Post-Christian Horizons." *Friends Journal* 10, no. 1 (January 1, 1964): 5–8.

Holmes, Jesse. "To the Scientifically-Minded." *Friends Intelligencer* 85, no. 6 (1928): 103–104. Reprinted in *Friends Journal* 38, no. 6 (June 1992): 22–23.

Holmes, Margaret. "What Have Quakers to Say to the Agnostic?" In Friends Home Service Committee, *In Search of God: Some Quaker Essays*. London: printed by author, 1966, pp. 14–20.

Ives, Kenneth H. *New Friends Speak: How and Why They Join Friends*. Studies in Quakerism 6. Chicago: Progresiv Publishr, 1980.

Ives, Kenneth H. *Recovering the Human Jesus*. Chicago: Progresiv Publishr, 1990.

Johnson, Eric. "Why I Am an Atheist." *Friends Journal* 37, no. 1 (January 1991): 17. Also in Quaker Universalist Fellowship. *Variations on the Quaker Message*. Pamphlet #201. Landenberg, PA: printed by author, 1991.

Johnson, Eric. "Atheism and Friends." Letter to the editor. *Friends Journal* 37, no. 5 (May 1991): 6.

Jones, Robinson. "A Great People to be Gathered." *The Universalist* 8 (July 1982): 27–34. Reprinted in Patricia A. Williams, ed. *Universalism and Religions*. Columbia MD: Quaker Universalist Fellowship, 2007, pp. 162–69.

Lacey, Paul. "The Death of 'the Man Upstairs': A Critical Appraisal of the New Theology." Comments by Chris Downing, J. H. McCandless and Clinton L. Reynolds, and response to comments by Paul Lacey. *Quaker Religious Thought* VIII, no. 1, issue #15 (1966): 3–36.

Linton, John. "Quakerism as Forerunner." *Friends Journal* 25, no. 17 (October 15, 1979): 4–9. Reprinted, Pamphlet #1. London: Quaker Universalist Group, 1979. Also reprinted in Quaker Universalist Fellowship. *The Quaker Universalist Reader Number 1: A Collection of Essays, Addresses and Lectures*. Landenberg, PA: printed by author, 1986, 1–13.

Linton, John. "Nothing Divides Us." *The Universalist* 12 (July 1984): 16–20.

Loukes, Harold and H. J. Blackham. *Humanists and Quakers: An Exchange of Letters*. London: Friends Home Service Committee, 1969.

Macmurray, John. *Search for Reality in Religion*. Swarthmore Lecture. London: George Allen & Unwin, 1965. Also published in London by Friends Home Service Committee, 1965, 1969 & 1984.

Mayer, Philip. *The Mature Spirit: Religion without Supernatural Hopes*. Northampton MA: Pittenprauch Press, 1987.

Miles, Thomas R. *Towards Universalism*. Pamphlet #7. London: Quaker Universalist Group, 1985. Reprinted in 1994.

Miller, Jr., Lawrence McK. "The 'Honest to God' Debate and Friends." *Friends Journal* 10, no. 6 (March 15, 1964): 124–26.

Morgan, Robert M. "Some Surprises For Us?" *Friends Journal* 22, no. 19 (November 15, 1976): 582–83.

Morgan, Robert M. and Claire Walker. "Toward New Concepts of God." *Friends Journal* 22, no. 19 (November 15, 1976): pp. 582–87. This includes a brief introduction and the articles listed here as Morgan (1976), Walker (1976), and Workshop for Non-Theistic Friends (1976).

Murphy, Carol. "Friends and Unbelievers." *Friends Journal* 11, no. 7 (April 1, 1965): 160–61.

Smith, Bradford. "Divine Law." *Friends Journal* 10, no. 13 (July 1, 1964), p. 292.

Smith, Bradford. "The Doubters." Poem. *Friends Journal* 11, no. 7 (April 1, 1965): 161.

Swayne, Kingdon W. "Confessions of a Post–Christian Agnostic." *Friends Journal* 26, no. 3 (March 15, 1980): 6–9. Also in Quaker Universalist Fellowship. *Variations on the Quaker Message*. Landenberg, PA: printed by author, 1990, 1–6.

Swayne, Kingdon W. "Humanist Philosophy as a Religious Resource," in Quaker Universalist Fellowship. *Varieties of Religious Experience: An Adventure In Listening*. Pamphlet #7. Landenberg PA: printed by author, 1990.

Swayne, Kingdon W. "Universalism and Me—3 Friends Respond." *Universalist Friends* 23 (1994): 9–10.

Walker, Claire. "Must We Feel Comfortable?" *Friends Journal* 9, no. 15 (August 1, 1963): 334.

Walker, Claire. "The Anti-Anthros Speak Out." *Friends Journal* 22, no. 19 (November 15, 1976): 583–85.

Williams, Jonathan. *My Quaker-Atheist Friend*. Poem about Basil Bunting. London: L. and R. Wallrich, 1973.

Recent Publications (1996–2013)

Alpern, Lincoln. "Testimony of a Nontheist Friend," in *Spirit Rising: Young Quaker Voices*. Philadelphia, PA: Quaker Press of Friends General Conference, 2010, 219–21.

Alpern, Robin. "Why Not Join the Unitarians?" *Universalist Friends*, 28 (1997): 23–28. Reprinted in Patricia A. Williams, ed. *Universalism and Religions*. Columbia MD: Quaker Universalist Fellowship, 2007, pp. 157–62. Also in *A Newsletter for Quakers of a Nontheistic Persuasion*, Michael Cox, ed., issue 1 (Fall 1996).

Alpern, Robin. "Meeting for Worship: an Opportunity for Being." Unpublished manuscript, 2006. http://www.nontheistfriends .org.

Alpern, Robin. "Reflections on a Decade of Nontheism Workshops." Unpublished manuscript, 2007. http://www.nontheistfriends .org.

Alpern, Robin. "Atheology", *Spark: New York Yearly Meeting News* 40, no. 4 (September 2009). Revised version of Robin Alpern, "What's a Nice Nontheist Like You Doing Here?" in David Boulton, ed., *Godless for God's Sake: Nontheism in Contemporary Quakerism*. Dent, Cumbria, UK: Dales Historical Monographs, 2006, pp. 17–26.

Amoss, Jr., George. "The Making of a Quaker Atheist." *Quaker Theology* 1 (1999): 55–62. http://www.quest.quaker.org. Also see James and Amoss (2000), below.

Anderson, Paul. "Is 'Nontheist Quakerism' a Contradiction of Terms?" In an issue of QRT titled "Quakers and Theism/Nontheism." *Quaker Religious Thought* 118 (2012): 5–24.

Arnold, Peter. "Keeping an open mind." Unpublished manuscript, 2005. http://www.nontheistfriends.org.

Bates, Paul. "Quaker Diversity." Talk given at the Frederick Street Meeting, Belfast, Ireland, November 24, 2013. http://www. nontheist-quakers.org.uk.

Boulton, David. *A Reasonable Faith: Introducing the Sea of Faith Newtwork*. Loughborough, England: Sea of Faith Network, 1996. http://www.sofn.org.uk.

Boulton, David. *The Faith of a Quaker Humanist*. Pamphlet #26. London: Quaker Universalist Group, 1997.

Boulton, David. *Gerard Winstanley and the Republic of Heaven*.
Dent, Cumbria, UK: Dales Historical Monographs, 1999.

Boulton, David. *Real Like the Daisies or Real Like I Love You? Essays in Radical Quakerism*. Dent, Cumbria, England: Dales Historical Monographs with Quaker Universalist Group, 2002.

Boulton, David. *The Trouble with God: Building the Republic of Heaven*, expanded edition. Winchester UK and Washington US: John Hunt Publishing, 2005.

Boulton, David, ed. *Godless for God's Sake: Nontheism in Contemporary Quakerism*. Dent, Cumbria, UK: Dales Historical Monographs, 2006 (contributors: Bowen Alpern, Lincoln Alpern, Robin Alpern, David Boulton, Anita Bower, Miriam Branson, Os Cresson, Joanna Dales, David E. Drake, Anne Filiaci, Philip Gross, David B. Lawrence, Joan Lukas, Tim Miles, Gudde (Gudrun) Moller, Hubert J. Morel-Seytoux, Sandy Parker, James T Dooley Riemermann, Elaine Ruscetta, David Rush, Kitty Rush, Jo Schlesinger, Marian Kaplun Shapiro, Wilmer Stratton, Carolyn Nicholson Terrell, Jeanne Warren and Beth Wray).

Boulton, David. "Godless for God's Sake: Demystifying Mysticism." *The Universalist* 77 (June 2006) 14. Reprinted in Patricia A. Williams, ed. *Universalism and Religions*. Columbia MD: Quaker Universalist Fellowship, 2007, pp. 169–174.

Boulton, David. *Who on Earth was Jesus? The Modern Quest for the Jesus of History*. Winchester, UK and Blue Ridge Summit, PA: O Books / John Hunt Publishing, 2008.

Boulton, David. "Nontheism Among Friends: Its Emergence and Meaning." In an issue of QRT titled "Quakers and Theism/Nontheism." *Quaker Religious Thought* 118 (2012): 35–44.

Britton, David. "Knowing Experimentally." *Friends Journal* 56, no. 10 (October 2010): 5.

Britton, Liberty. "Identity Creation: Nontheist Quaker." Unpublished manuscript, 2011. http://www.nontheistfriends.org.

Cadbury, Henry J. "My Personal Religion." Lecture given at Harvard Divinity School, 1936. Published in *Universalist Friends* 35(Fall–

Winter 2000): 22–31, with corrections in *Universalist Friends* 36 (Spring–Summer 2001): 18.

Craigo-Snell, Shannon. "Response to David Boulton and Jeffrey Dudiak." In an issue of QRT titled "Quakers and Theism/Nontheism." *Quaker Religious Thought* 118 (2012): 45–50.

Cresson, Os. "Sharing Meeting." *Friends Journal* 47, no. 1 (January 2001): 5.

Cresson, Os. "Quaker in a Material World." *Quaker Theology* 5, no. 1 (Spring–Summer 2003): 23–54. http://quest.quaker.org.

Cresson, Os. "Quakers and the Environment: Three Options. Unpublished manuscript, 2005. http://www.nontheistfriends.org.

Cresson, Os. "Quakers from the Viewpoint of a Naturalist." *Friends Journal* 52, no. 3 (March 2006): 18–20.

Cresson, Os. "On Quaker Unity." *Friends Journal* 55, no. 7 (July 2009): 5.

Cresson, Os. "Doctrinally Open Membership in the Religious Society of Friends." Unpublished manuscript, 2010. http://www.nontheistfriends.org.

Cresson, Os. "Listening and Speaking from the Heart." *Friends Journal* 59, no. 5 (May 2013): 5.

Drake, David E. "Confessions of a Nontheistic Friend." *Friends Journal* 49, no. 6 (June 2003): 18–20.

Dudiak, Jeffrey. "Quakers and Theism/Nontheism: Questions and Prospects." In an issue of *QRT* titled "Quakers and Theism/Nontheism." *Quaker Religious Thought* 118 (2012): 25–34.

Earp, Charley. "In Search of Religious Radicalism." *Quaker Theology*, no. 11 (2005). http://quest.quaker.org.

Fager, Chuck. Review of *Godless for God's Sake: Nontheism in Contemporary Quakerism*, ed. by David Boulton. *Quaker Theology* 7, no. 2 (winter 2007). http://www.quest.quaker.org.

Friends at Twin Cities Friends Meeting. "Statement on Theological Diversity" *Universalist Friends* 43 (February 2006) 23. Reprinted as "Theological Diversity Within Twin Cities Meeting" in Patricia

A. Williams, ed. *Universalism and Religions*. Columbia MD: Quaker Universalist Fellowship, 2007, pp. 174–76.

Furry, Susan. "Recognizing That of God in Each Other." *Friends Journal* 53, no. 3 (March 2007): 5.

Gjelfriend, George. "Useful Fictions." *Friends Journal* 53, no. 8 (August 2007): 19.

Grundy, Martha Paxson. Review of *Godless for God's Sake: Nontheism in Contemporary Quakerism*, by 27 Quaker nontheists, ed. by David Boulton. *Friends Journal* 52 (November 2006): 25–26.

Hoare, Edward. "Time to Speak Out." *The Friend* (October 16, 2009), http://www.thefriend.org.

Holmes, Jesse. "'Our Christianity'?" *Universalist Friends* 39 (Fall & Winter, 2003): 15–22.

Hughes, Ian. "Is Quakerism a 'Religion For Atheists'? Review of Alain De Botton (2012) *Religion for Atheists*. London: Hamish Hamilton." *Australian Friend* 12, no. 6 (June 2012) http://australianfriend.org.

Ives, Kenneth H. *Some Quaker Perspectives for the Years 2000+*. Chicago: Progresiv Publishr, 1996.

James, Edward and George Amoss Jr. "An Exchange: Quaker Theology Without God?" *Quaker Theology* 2, no. 1 (Spring 2000). http://www.quest.quaker.org.

Kuenning, Larry. Review of *Speaking of God: Theism, Atheism and the Magnus Image* by T. R. Miles. *Quaker Religious Thought* 29(1) (1998): 42–43.

Lukas, Joan. "What Do I Do in Meeting? The Experience of a Nontheist Quaker." Unpublished manuscript prepared for forum held at Friends Meeting at Cambridge, May 9, 2004.

Mason, Marcia L. "Journey of a Doubter." *Friends Journal* 57, no. 9 (September 2011).

Miles, Thomas R. *Speaking of God: Theism, Atheism and the Magnus Image*. York, UK: William Sessions, 1998.

Morgan, Arthur. *Should Quakers Receive the Good Samaritan Into*

Their Membership? Landenberg, PA: Quaker Universalist Fellowship, 1998.

Nugent, Patrick J. "Response to Papers on Theism (Just a Little) and Non-Theism (Much More)." In an issue of *QRT* titled "Quakers and Theism/Nontheism." *Quaker Religious Thought* 118 (2012): 51–56.

Reed, Jessica. "Quakerism: Sharing Your Religion." *The Friend* (January 20, 2010), http://www.thefriend.org.

Riemermann, James. "One God at Most, or Two Gods at Least?" Unpublished manuscript, 2006. http://www.nontheistfriends .org.

Riemermann, James. "What is a Nontheist?" Unpublished manuscript, 2006. http://www.nontheistfriends.org.

Riemermann, James. *Mystery: It's What We Don't Know*. Quaker Universalist Fellowship Pamphlets, 2008. http://www.universal istfriends.org. Also in David Boulton, ed., *Godless for God's Sake: Nontheism in Contemporary Quakerism*. Dent, Cumbria, UK: Dales Historical Monographs, 2006, pp. 43–51.

Riemermann, James. "Revealing our True Selves." Paper presented at conference of Nontheist Friends Network, Birmingham, UK, March 2012. http://www.nontheistfriends.org.

Rush, David. "They Too Are Quakers: A Survey of 199 Nontheist Friends." *The Woodbrooke Journal* 11 (Winter 2002). Reprinted as "They Too Are Quakers: A Survey of 199 Nontheist Friends." Millsboro, VA: Quaker Universalist Fellowship, 2003.

Seeger, Daniel A. "Why Do the Unbelievers Rage? The New Atheists and the Universality of the Light." *Friends Journal* 56, no. 1 (January 2010): 6–11.

Seltman, Muriel. *Bread and Roses: Nontheism and the Human Spirit*. Kibworth Beauchamp, UK: Matador, 2013.

Smith, Steve. "'Leadings' For Nontheistic Friends?" *Friends Journal* 57, no. 1 (January 2011): 22–25.

Stern, T. Noel. "How I Became a Universalist Quaker." *Universalist Friends* 37 (Fall & Winter 2002): 21–31.

Vura-Weis, Brian. "Quakers & Non-Theism." *Western Friend* (July/August, 2009).

Wise, Julia. "No Religion. Always Practicing Quakerism." *Friends Journal* 58, no. 4 (April 2012): 26.

Wright, Michael. "Disagreeing About God." *The Friend* (October 18, 2013).

Yagud, Miriam. "The Wrong Silence." *The Friend* 169, no. 5 (February 4, 2011): 14.

Publications by Nontheist Friends Gatherings

Boulton, David, David Rush, and Kitty Rush. "Minute." Minute approved by the workshop, "Beyond Universalism: The Experience and Understanding of Nontheism in Contemporary Quakerism," held at Woodbrooke Quaker Study Centre, Birmingham, UK, January 9–11, 2004. http://www.nontheistfriends.org. Also in "Quaker Non-Theism," by David Boulton, *The Friend* (February 20, 2004): 15, and described in "News" by David Boulton, David Rush, and Kitty Rush, *Friends Journal* 50, no.7 (July 2004): 39.

Conference of the Nontheist Friends Network, 2012. "Minute and Epistle." Minute approved by "Nontheism Among Friends," the inaugural conference of the Nontheist Friends Network held at Woodbrooke Quaker Study Centre, Birmingham, UK, March 9–11, 2012. http://www.nontheist-quakers.org.uk.

Conference of the Nontheist Friends Network, 2013. "Minute and Epistle." Minute approved by "Nontheism Among Friends," the 2nd annual conference of the Nontheist Friends Network held at Woodbrooke Quaker Study Centre, Birmingham, UK, March 1–3, 2013. http://www.nontheistfriends.org.

Gathering of Nontheist Friends at Woodbrooke Quaker Study Centre. "Minute and Epistle." Approved by the workshop, "What Next for Quaker Nontheism," held at Woodbrooke

Quaker Study Centre, Birmingham, UK, February 18–20, 2011. http://www.nontheistfriends.org.

Workshop for Non-Theistic Friends. "Seekers Beyond Tradition." *Friends Journal* 22, no. 19 (November 15, 1976): 586–87. Slightly edited version of unpublished report by participants in the Workshop for Non-Theistic Friends held at the Friends General Conference Gathering, Ithaca NY, June 26–July 3, 1976. http://www.nontheistfriends.org. Workshop also described in Robert Morgan (1976), above.

Workshop on "Quaker Identity and the Heart of our Faith." "Minute." Approved by the workshop, "Quaker Identity and the Heart of our Faith," held at the Friends General Conference Gathering, Blacksburg VA, June 26–July 4, 2009. http://www.nontheistfriends.org.

Bibliography

Resource material for the people mentioned in
Roots and Flowers of Quaker Nontheism

Anthony, Susan B.

Anthony, Katharine. *Susan B. Anthony: Her Personal History and Her Era.* NY: Doubleday, 1954.

Barry, Kathleen. *Susan B. Anthony: A Biography of a Singular Feminist.* NY: New York University Press, 1988.

Sherr, Lynn. *Failure is Impossible: Susan B. Anthony In Her Own Words.* NY: Random House, 1995.

Jacob Bauthumley

Bauthumley, Jacob. *The Light and Dark Sides of God .* London: William Learner, 1650. Also in Nigel Smith. *A Collection of Ranter Writings from the 17th Century.* London: Junction Books, 1983.

Cohn, Norman. *The Pursuit of the Millennium*: *Revolutionary Millenarians and Mystical Anarchists of the Middle Ages.* New York: Oxford University Press, 1970.

Hill, Christopher. *The World Turned Upside Down: Radical Ideas During the English Revolution.* NY: Viking Press, 1972.

Barnard, Hannah

American National Biography, s.v. "Barnard, Hannah Jenkins."

Barnard, Hannah. *Dialogues on Domestic and Rural Economy, and Fashionable Follies of the World. Interspersed with Occasional Observations on Some Popular Opinions. To Which is Added an Appendix, on Burns, etc. with their Treatment.* Hudson, NY: Samuel W. Clark, 1820.

Cresson, Os. "Hannah Barnard's Story." Unpublished manuscript, 2006.

Fager, Chuck. "Hannah Barnard—A Liberal Quaker Hero."
Friends Journal 42 no. 1 (1996): 11–12.

Frost, J. William. *The Records and Recollections of James Jenkins*. Texts and Studies in Religion, Vol. 18. NY: Edwin Mellen
Press, 1984, pp. 339–80.

Maxey, David. "New Light on Hannah Barnard, A Quaker 'Heretic'," *Quaker History* (Fall, 1989): 61–86.

Bartram, John

Clarke, Larry R. "The Quaker Background of William Bartram's
View of Nature." *Journal of the History of Ideas* 46, no. 3
(1985): 435–448.

Darlington, William and Peter Collinson, eds. *Memorials of John
Bartram and Humphrey Marshall*. NY: Hafner, 1967.

Wilson, David Scofield. *In the Presence of Nature*. Amherst MA:
University of Massachusetts Press, 1978.

Bean, Hannah and Joel

Bean, Joel. "The Issue." *British Friend* (March 1881): 49–51.

Fager, Chuck. *Without Apology*. Bellefonte PA: Kimo Press, 1996.

Le Shana, David. *Quakers in California*. Newberg, OR: Barclay
Press, 1969.

Brady, George S.

Brady, George S. *Lumen Siccum (An Essay on the Exercise of the
Intellect in Matters of Religious Belief*. London: F. Bowyer
Kitto, 1869.

Brady, George S. "State of the Society of Friends," *Manchester
Friend*. 2, no. 10 (Oct. 15, 1873): 168.

Brady, George S. "Editorial Comments." *Manchester Friend*. 1,
no. 7 (June 15, 1872): 97–98.

Burtt, E. A.

Burtt, E. A. *Types of Religious Philosophy*, rev. edn. NY: Harper &
Row, 1957.

Burtt, E. A. *Teachings of the Compassionate Buddha*. NY: New American Library, 1955/1982.

Burtt, E. A. *In Search of Philosophic Understanding*. NY: New American Library, 1965.

Burtt, E. A. *Light, Love and Life*. Ithaca NY: Cayuga Press, 1988.

Burtt, E. A. "God," "Love," and "The Human Journey Toward and Beyond a World Community." Three unpublished essays at Friends Historical Library of Swarthmore College, Mary R. Hopkins Papers, 1936–1998, RG5/222; the first two dated June 1980, the other undated.

Villemaire, Diane. E. A. Burtt: *Historian and Philosopher: A Study of the Author of The Metaphysical Foundations of Modern Science*. Dordrecht and London: Kluwar Academic Publishers, 2002.

Cadbury, Henry J.

Bacon, Margaret Hope. *Let This Life Speak: The Legacy of Henry Joel Cadbury*. Philadelphia: University of Pennsylvania Press, 1987.

Bacon, Margaret Hope. *Henry J. Cadbury: Scholar, Activist, Disciple*. Pamphlet #376. Wallingford, PA: Pendle Hill, 2005.

Cadbury, Henry J. "My Personal Religion." *Universalist Friends* 35 (Fall-Winter 2000): 22–31, with corrections in 36 (Spring-Summer 2000): 18.

Cadbury, Henry J. *Quakerism and Early Christianity*. London: Allen & Unwin, 1957.

Cadbury, Henry J. *The Character of A Quaker*. Pamphlet #103. Wallingford, PA: Pendle Hill, 1959. Also in "Two Strands in Quakerism." *Friends Journal* 14, no. 5 (April 4, 1959): 212–14.

Cadbury, Henry J. "My Religious Pilgrimage." (Notes for talk at Doylestown Monthly Meeting, April 1, 1962.) Unpublished manuscript, 1962. Henry J. Cadbury Papers, Quaker Collection, Haverford College, Haverford, PA.

Cadbury, Henry J. "Quakerism and/or Christianity." *Friends Bulletin* 35, no. 4 (1966): 1–10.

Cresson, Os. "Henry Joel Cadbury: No Assurance of God or Immortality" in Boulton, David, ed. *Godless for God's Sake: Nontheism in Contemporary Quakerism.* Dent, Cumbria, UK: Dales Historical Monographs, 2006, pp.85–90.

Duncan, David

Cresson, Os. "David Duncan and the Free Friends of Manchester" in Boulton, David, ed. *Godless for God's Sake: Nontheism in Contemporary Quakerism.* Dent, Cumbria, UK: Dales Historical Monographs, 2006, pp. 82–85 & 90.

Duncan, David. *'Essays and Reviews'. A Lecture.* Manchester, UK, 1861.

Duncan, David. *Can an Outward Revelation be Perfect? Reflections upon the Claim of Biblical Infallibility.* London, 1871.

Isichei, Elizabeth. *Victorian Quakers.* Oxford: Oxford University Press, 1970.

Kennedy, Thomas. *British Quakerism 1860–1920.* Oxford: Oxford University Press, 2001.

Eddington, Arthur S.

Eddington, Arthur S. *Science and the Unseen World.* NY: Macmillan, 1930.

Forster, Joseph B.

Forster, Joseph B. *On Liberty: An Address to Members of the Society of Friends,* 1867. Quoted in Isichei, *Victorian Quakers,* 30.

Forster, Joseph B. *The Society of Friends and Freedom of Thought in 1871,* 1871.

Manchester Friend. Ed. Joseph B. Forster, 1871–73.

Free Quakers

Wetherill, Charles. *History of the Free Quakers.* Washington. D.C.: Ross & Perry, 2002.

Wetherill, Samuel. *An Address To those of the People called Quakers, who have been disowned for Matters Religious and Civil.* Philadelphia, PA, 1781. Reprinted in Wetherill, *History of the Free Quakers,* above, pp. 47–49.

Hicks, Elias

Forbush, Bliss. *Elias Hicks: Quaker Liberal*. NY: Columbia University Press, 1956.

Jacob, Norma. *Introducing. . . .Elias Hicks: A Condensation of Bliss Forbush's Original Biography*. Philadelphia: Friends General Conference, 1984.

Holmes, Jesse H.

Holmes, Jesse. *The Modern Message of Quakerism*. Philadelphia: Friends General Conference, 1912. Also published as *What is Truth?* Philadelphia: Friends General Conference (undated).

Holmes, Jesse. "To the Scientifically-Minded." *Friends Intelligencer* 85, no. 6 (1928): 103–04. Reprinted in *Friends Journal* 38, no. 6 (June 1992): 22–23. Also published as *To the Scientifically-Minded*. Philadelphia: Friends General Conference (undated), and *A Los Intelectuales*. Philadelphia: Friends General Conference (undated).

Holmes, Jesse. "The Quakers and the Sciences." *Friends Intelligencer* 88, no. 6 (1931): 537–38.

Holmes, Jesse. "'Our Christianity'?" *Universalist Friends* 39 (Fall & Winter, 2003): 15–22.

Stern, T. Noel. "Jesse Holmes, Liberal Quaker." *Friends Journal* 38, no. 6 (June 1992): 21–23.

Wahl, Albert J. *Jesse Herman Holmes, 1864–1942: A Quaker's Affirmation for Man*. Richmond, IN: Friends United Press, 1979.

Humanist Society of Friends (Lowell H. Coate)

The Humanist Friend, 1939–1944.

Wilson, Edwin H. *Genesis of a Humanist Manifesto*, Amherst NY: Humanist Press, 1995.

Johnson, Eric

Johnson, Eric. "Why I Am an Atheist." *Friends Journal* 37, no. 1 (January 1991): 17. Also in Quaker Universalist Fellowship. *Variations on the Quaker Message*. Pamphlet #201. Landenberg, PA: printed by author, 1991.

Johnson, Eric. "Atheism and Friends." Letter to the editor. *Friends Journal* 37, no. 5 (May 1991): 6.

Linton, John

Linton, John. "A Universalist Group." Letter to the editor. *The Friend.* 136 (April 21, 1978): 484.

Linton, John. "A Universalist Group." Letter to the editor. *The Friend.* 136 (October 20, 1978): 1315.

Linton, John. "Quakerism as Forerunner." *Friends Journal* 25, no. 17 (October 15, 1979): 4–9. Reprinted as *Quakerism as Forerunner.* Pamphlet #1. London: Quaker Universalist Group, 1979. Also reprinted in Quaker Universalist Fellowship. *The Quaker Universalist Reader Number 1: A Collection of Essays, Addresses and Lectures.* Landenberg, PA: printed by author, 1986, 1–13.

Linton, John. "Nothing Divides Us." *The Universalist* 12 (1984): 16–20.

Littleboy, William

Littleboy, William. *The Appeal of Quakerism to the Non-Mystic.* Harrowgate, England: Committee of Yorkshire Quarterly Meeting of the Society of Friends, 1916. Reprinted by the Friends Literature Committee, Yorkshire, 1938, and by Friends Book Centre, London, 1945.

Lynd, Alice and Staughton

Lynd, Alice and Staughton Lynd. *Liberation Theology for Quakers.* Pamphlet #326. Walingford, PA: Pendle Hill, 1996. Reprinted in Lynd, Staughton, *Living Inside our Hope,* below.

Lynd, Staughton. *Living Inside our Hope: A Steadfast Radical's Thoughts on Rebuilding the Movement.* Ithaca, NY: Cornell University Press, 1997.

Mitchell, Maria

Albers, Henry, ed. *Maria Mitchell: A Life in Journals and Letters.* Clinton Corners, NY: College Avenue Press, 2001.

Brackett, Anna C. "Maria Mitchell", *The Century* 38, no. 6 (1889): 954.

Kendall, Phebe Mitchell. *Maria Mitchell: Life, Letters and Journals.* Boston: Lee and Shepard, 1896. Reprinted by Classic Textbooks.

Morgan, Helen. *Maria Mitchell, First Lady of American Astronomy.* Philadelphia: Westminster Press, 1977.

Wright, Helen. *Sweeper in the Sky: The Life of Maria Mitchell, First Woman Astronomer in America.* NY: Macmillan, 1949.

Mitchell, Morris

Mitchell, Morris. *World Education—Revolutionary Concept.* NY: Pageant Press, 1967.

Sobel, Bart. "Morris Mitchell: Prophet of World Education." PhD diss., Boston University, 1971. University Microfilms, Ann Arbor, MI.

Morgan, Arthur

Kahoe, Walter. *Arthur Morgan: A Biography and Memoir.* Moylan, PA: The Whimsie Press, 1977.

Morgan, Arthur. "My World." Unpublished manuscript, 1927. Library, Antioch College, Yellow Springs, OH.

Morgan, Arthur. *Should Quakers Receive the Good Samaritan Into Their Membership?* Landenberg, PA: Quaker Universalist Fellowship, 1998.

Morgan, Arthur. *Search for Purpose.* Yellow Springs, OH: Community Service, Inc., 1957.

Morgan, Arthur. "Necessity." Unpublished manuscript, 1968. Quoted in Kahoe, *Arthur Morgan,* above.

Morgan, Ernest. *Arthur Morgan Remembered.* Yellow Springs, OH: Community Service, Inc., 1991.

Wilson, Edwin H. *Genesis of a Humanist Manifesto.* Amherst, NY: Humanist Press, 1995.

Mott, Lucretia

Bacon, Margaret Hope. *Valiant Friend: The Life of Lucretia Mott.* NY: Walker and Company, 1980. Reprinted in Philadelphia: Friends General Conference, 1999.

Cromwell, Otilia. *Lucretia Mott*. Cambridge, MA: Harvard University Press, 1958.

Greene, Dana, ed. *Lucretia Mott: Her Complete Speeches and Sermons*. NY: Edwin Mellen Press, 1980.

Hallowell, Anna Davis. *James and Lucretia Mott. Life and Letters.* Boston: Houghton, Mifflin, 1890.

Palmer, Beverly Wilson, ed. *Selected Letters of Lucretia Coffin Mott*. Urbana: University of Illinois Press, 2002.

New Lights of New England

Tolles, Frederick B. "The New-Light Quakers of Lynn and New Bedford" *The New England Quarterly* 32, no. 3 (September 1959): 291–319.

Peters, Richard S.

Peters, Richard S. *Ethics and Education*, 5th edn. London: George Allen & Unwin, 1968.

Peters, Richard S. *Reason, Morality and Religion*. Swarthmore Lecture. London: Friends Home Service Committee, 1972. Also in Richard S. Peters. *Reason and Compassion*. London and Boston: Routledge & K. Paul, 1973.

Peters, Richard S. *Authority, Responsibility and Education*, 3rd edn. London: George Allen & Unwin, 1973.

Progressive Friends at Longwood

Densmore, Christopher. "Be Ye Therefore Perfect: Anti-Slavery and the Origins of the Yearly Meeting of Progressive Friends in Chester County, Pennsylvania." *Quaker History* 93, no. 2 (Fall 2004): 28–46.

Longwood Progressive Friends Meetinghouse, 1855–1940: 150 Anniversary Celebration. Kennett Square, PA, May 22, 2005.

Rowntree, Joseph

Rowntree, Joseph. *Memorandum on the Declaration of Christian Doctrine issued by the Richmond Conference, 1887*. York, UK, 5th month 10, 1888.

Seeger, Daniel A.

Bien, Peter and Chuck Fager, eds. In Stillness There is Fullness:

A Peacemaker's Harvest: Essays and Reflections in Honor of
Daniel A. Seeger's Four Decades of Quaker Service. Bellefonte,
PA: Kimo Press, 2000.

Cresson, Os. "Reviews of Publications on Quaker Nontheism in
the 1960s." (Review #4.) Unpublished manuscript. Online at
www.nontheistfriends.org.

Seeger, Daniel A. "Is Coexistence Possible?" Friends Journal 30,
no. 12 (1984): 11–14. Also in Quaker Universalist Fellowship.
Quaker Universalist Reader Number 1. Laudenberg, PA: printed
by author, 1986, 85.

Seeger, Daniel A. The Mystical Path: Pilgrimage To The One Who
Is Always Here. Millboro, VA: Quaker Universalist Fellowship,
2004. Online at www.universalistfriends.org.

Seeger, Daniel A. "Why Do the Unbelievers Rage: The New Atheists and the Universality of the Light." Friends Journal 56, no. 1
(Jan. 1, 2010): 6–11. Online at www.friendsjournal.org.

Shackleton, Abraham

Grubb, Mollie. "Abraham Shackleton and the Irish Separation
of 1797–1803." Journal of the Friends Historical Society 56, no.
4 (1993): 262–271.

Stanton, Elizabeth Cady

Densmore, Christopher. "Forty-Seven Years Before the Woman's
Bible: Elizabeth Cady Stanton and the Congregational Friends."
Paper presented at the Women's Centennial Conference, Sene-
ca Falls, NY, November 4, 1995. By courtesy of the author.

DuBois, Ellen. The Elizabeth Cady Stanton-Susan B. Anthony Reader. Ithaca NY: Cornell University Press, 1994.

Gaylor, Annie Laurie. Women Without Superstition: No Gods—No
Masters. Madison WI: Freedom From Religion Foundation,
1997.

Stanton, Elizabeth Cady. Eighty Years & More: Reminiscences
1815–1897. Boston: Northeastern University Press, 1993.

Stanton, Elizabeth Cady. The Woman's Bible. Boston: Northeastern University Press, 1993.

Stanton, Theodore and Harriot Stanton Blatch, eds. *Elizabeth Cady Stanton As Revealed in Her Letters Diary and Reminiscences, Volumes One and Two*. NY: Arno & The New York Times, 1969.

Swayne, Kingdon W.

Swayne, Kingdon W. "Confessions of a Post-Christian Agnostic." *Friends Journal* 26, no. 3 (March 15, 1980): 6–9. Also in Quaker Universalist Fellowship. *Variations on the Quaker Message*. Landenberg, PA: printed by author, 1990, 1–6.

Swayne, Kingdon W. "Universalism or Latitudinarianism?" *Universalist Friends* 7 (1986): 8–11.

Swayne, Kingdon W. "Humanist Philosophy as a Religious Resource," in Quaker Universalist Fellowship. *Varieties of Religious Experience: An Adventure In Listening*. Pamphlet #7. Landenberg PA: printed by author, 1990.

Swayne, Kingdon W. "Universalism and Me—3 Friends Respond." *Universalist Friends* 23 (1994): 9–10.

Walker, Claire

Blalock, Heidi. "Remembering Claire." *Collection: The Magazine of Friends School of Baltimore* (Spring 2009), pp. 2–5. http://freepages.genealogy.rootsweb.ancestry.com/~mysong/exhibits/walker_claire_groben_collection2009.pdf.

Walker, Claire. "Must We Feel Comfortable?" *Friends Journal* 9, no. 15 (August 1, 1963): 334.

Walker, Claire. "The Anti-Anthros Speak Out." *Friends Journal* 22, no. 19 (November 15, 1976): 583–85.

Winstanley, Gerrard

Boulton, David. *Gerrard Winstanley and the Republic of Heaven*. Dent, Cumbria, UK: Dales Historical Monographs, 1999.

Boulton, David. *Militant Seedbeds of Early Quakerism*. Landenberg, PA: Quaker Universalist Fellowship, 2005. http://www.universalistfriends.org/boulton.html.

Cohn, Norman. *The Pursuit of the Millennium: Revolutionary*

Millenarians and Mystical Anarchists of the Middle Ages. NY: Oxford University Press, 1970.

Hill, Christopher. *The World Turned Upside Down: Radical Ideas During the English Revolution.* NY: Viking Press, 1972.

Sabine, George Holland. *The Works of Gerrard Winstanley.* New York: Russell & Russell, 1965.

Workshop for Non-Theistic Friends (Robert Morgan)

Morgan, Robert M. "Some Surprises For Us?" *Friends Journal* 22, no. 19 (November 15, 1976): 582–83.

Workshop for Non-Theistic Friends. "Seekers Beyond Tradition." *Friends Journal* 22, no. 19 (November 15, 1976): 586–87. Slightly edited version of unpublished report by participants in the Workshop for Non-Theistic Friends held at the Friends General Conference Gathering, Ithaca NY, June 26–July 3, 1976.

Source Notes

Listening and Speaking from the Heart: An Anthology

1. John Woolman, *The Journal of John Woolman* (Boston: Houghton Mifflin, 1871), 201.

2. Douglas Steere, *Gleanings: A Random Harvest* (Nashville TN: The Upper Room, 1986), 83.

3. Rachel Naomi Remen, in Andrea S. Cohen, Leah Green and Susan Partnow, *Practicing the Art of Compassionate Listening* (Indianola WA: The Compassionate Listening Project, 2011), 80.

4. Tom Gates, "Seeing Beyond Our Differences: Meeting as 'Covenant Community'," May 2008, italics in the original, http://lancaster paquakers.org/SITEdocs/CovenantRetreat.pdf.

5. Gene Knudsen-Hoffman, "Speaking Truth to Power," *Friends Journal* 27, no. 14 (October 1, 1981): 15.

6. George Lakey, "Connecting through Conflict," *FGConnections* (Summer 2007), http://schoolofthespirit.org.

7. Isaac Penington, *A Treatise Concerning God's Teaching,* in *The Works of Isaac Penington,* vol. 4 (Glenside PA: Quaker Heritage Press, 1997), 261.

8. Oliver Johnson, Message during yearly meeting in Waterloo NY, June 3, 1855, in the *Proceedings of the Annual Meeting of Friends of Human Progress* (Syracuse NY: Evening Chronicle Print, 1855), 5.

9. Thomas R. Kelly, *A Testament of Devotion* (NY: Harper Collins, 1996), 98.

10. Andrea S. Cohen, Leah Green and Susan Partnow, *Art of Compassionate Listening,* 13.

11. The Yearly Meeting of the Religious Society of Friends (Quak-

ers) in Britain, *Quaker Faith and Practice*, 4th ed. (London: printed by author, 2008), #3.10.

12. Isaac Penington, *The Works of Isaac Penington: A Minister of the Gospel in the Society of Friends: Including His Collected Letters*, vol. 1 (Glenside PA: Quaker Heritage, 1995).

13. Joseph B. Forster, editorial in *The Manchester Friend* 2, no. 12 (1873): 189.

14. The Yearly Meeting of the Religious Society of Friends (Quakers) in Britain, http://www.quaker.org.uk/quaker-beliefs.

15. Philadelphia Yearly Meeting, *Faith and Practice* (Philadelphia: printed by author, 2001), 36.

16. Parker J. Palmer, *A Place Called Community*, pamphlet #212 (Wallingford, PA: Pendle Hill, 1977), 27.

17. Arthur Morgan, *"Should Quakers Receive the Good Samaritan Into Their Membership?,"* talk at Shrewsbury and Plainfield Half-Yearly Meeting, March 27, 1954 (Landenberg, PA: Quaker Universalist Fellowship, 1998).

18. David Boulton, "The Diversity of Truth," in *Real Like the Daisies or Real Like I Love You? Essays in Radical Quakerism* (Dent, Cumbria, England: Dales Historical Monographs with Quaker Universalist Group, 2002), 33–38. Paper delivered to the Quaker Theology Seminar on "Truth and Diversity," Birmingham, UK, 1995. Also in Harvey Gillman and Alastair Heron, *Searching the Depths: Essays on Being a Quaker Today*, 2nd. ed. (London: Quaker Home Service, 1998), 27–36.

19. Tim Miles, *Towards Universalism*, pamphlet #7 (London: Quaker Universalist Group, 1985, reprinted 1994), http://www.qug.org.uk/MILES.pdf.

20. Henry J. Cadbury, "Quakerism and/or Christianity," *Friends Bulletin* 35, no. 4 (1966): 1–10.

21. Henry J. Cadbury, *Quakerism and Early Christianity* (London: Allen & Unwin, 1957), 47–48.

22. Daniel A. Seeger, *Sharing Our Faith: Christian and Universalist Aspects of Friends Spiritual Experience* (Philadelphia: Friends General Conference, 1991), 7.

23. Margery Post Abbott, *An Experiment in Faith: Quaker Women Transcending Differences,* pamphlet #323 (Wallingford, PA: Pendle Hill, 1995), 25–26, italics in the original.

24. The Yearly Meeting of the Religious Society of Friends (Quakers) in Britain, *Quaker Faith and Practice* (London: printed by author, 1995), 17.

25. Ben Pink Dandelion, "Quaking with Confidence," *Friends Journal* 55, no. 12 (December 2009). 12–17.

26. Howard Brinton, "The Kind of Paper We Want", *The Friend* (December 23, 1954): 197.

27. Henry J. Cadbury, "Vital Issues for Friends Today," *Canadian Friend* 60, no. 3 (1964): 3–4.

28. Rex Ambler, "Quaker Identity: Anything Goes?," *The Friends Quarterly* 31, no. 8 (1997): 371–80.

29. David Boulton, *The Diversity of Truth*, 27–36.

30. Anthony Manousos, "Are Quakers Christian, Non-Christian, or Both?," *Friends Journal* 59, no. 2 (February 2013): 19–22.

31. James Riemermann. "Revealing our True Selves" (paper presented at conference of Nontheist Friends Network, Birmingham UK, March 2012), http://www.nontheistfriends.org.

Science Is . . .

32. B. F. Skinner, *Cumulative Record* (Cambridge MA: B. F. Skinner Foundation, 1999), 370.

33. Ernst Mach, *The Science of Mechanics: A Critical and Historical Account of its Development,* 4th ed. (Chicago: Open Court, 1919), 496, italics in the original.

34. Bertrand Russell, *Why I Am Not a Christian and Other Essays on Religion and Related Subjects* (NY: Simon and Schuster, 1957), 6–7.

35. (a) Robert T. Pennock, ed., *Intelligent Design Creationism and Its Critics : Philosophical, Theological, and Scientific Perspectives* (Cambridge, MA: MIT Press, 2001), 84–85. Also in Robert T. Pennock, *Tower of Babel: The Evidence Against the New Creationism* (Cambridge, MA:

MIT Press, 1999), 191. See *"Naturalism," Stanford Encyclopedia of Phi-losophy,* http://plato.stanford.edu. Also see "Medthodological Natural-ism," Wikipedia, http://wikipedia.org. (b) Robert T. Pennock, *Kitzmiller, et al. v. Dover Area School District-Expert Report,* https://www.msu.edu. See "Judgment Day: Intelligent Design on Trial," PBS NOVA television program, # WG41699, Nov. 13, 2007, http://www.pbs.org.

36. B. F. Skinner, *Science and Human Behavior* (Cambridge: B. F. Skin-ner Foundation, 2005), 13.

37. Ludwig Wittgenstein, *Tractatus Logico-Philosophicus* (NY: Hu-manities Press, 1961), 151.

38. B. F. Skinner, *Science and Human Behavior* (Cambridge MA: B. F. Skinner Foundation, 2005), 449.

39. Alan Watts, "The Individual as Man/World," *The Psychedelic Re-view* 1, no. 1 (1963): 55–65, http://www.lycaeum.org/leda/docs/16422 .shtml.

40. Lao Tzu, *Tao Te Ching: A New English Version*, trans. Stephen Mitchell (NY: HarperCollins, 1988), Chapter 1.

41. Percy W. Bridgman, *The Logic of Modern Physics* (NY: Macmillan, 1927), 5.

42. B. F. Skinner, "On 'Having' a Poem," *The Saturday Review* (July 15, 1972): 32–35.

43. B. F. Skinner, "The Operational Analysis of Psychological Terms," *Psychological Review* 52 (1945): 270–77.

44. Luke 11:39–40; Matt. 23:25–26; Thom. 89.

45. Henry J. Cadbury, "My Personal Religion," *Universalist Friends* 35 (Fall-Winter 2000): 22–31, with corrections in 36 (Spring-Summer 2000): 18.

46. Philip Clayton, Mary Coelho, and The New Story Study Group, *Quakers and the New Story: Essays on Science and Spirituality* (Cam-bridge MA: The New Story Study Group, Friends Meeting at Cambridge, 2007). Also published by Quaker Earthcare Witness as a PDF Book-let, http://www.quakerearthcare.org. See Mary Coelho, *Awakening Universe, Emerging Personhood: The Power of Contemplation in an Evolving Universe* (Bristol, IN: Wyndham Hall, 2002).

47. Doris Ferm, *Beyond Stewardship of Nature: Friends and the Great Story* (Philadelphia, PA: The Wider Quaker Fellowship, 2011).

48. Murray Sidman, Osborne Cresson, Jr., and Martha Willson-Morris, "Acquisition of matching to sample via mediated transfer," *Journal of the Experimental Analysis of Behavior* 22 (1974): 261–73.

49. Kenneth Boulding, "Science as a Quaker Testimony," *Pendle Hill Bulletin* #369 (1989).

50. Howard Brinton, *Friends For 350 Years* (Wallingford PA: Pendle Hill, 2002), 32 and 37.

51. (a) Elizabeth Gray Vining, *Friend of Life: The Biography of Rufus M. Jones* (Philadelphia, PA: Philadelphia Yearly Meeting, 1958). See Mary Hoxie Jones, *Rufus M. Jones* (London: Friends Home Service Committee, 1970), and Claus Bernet, *Rufus Jones (1863–1948): Life and Bibliography of an American Scholar, Writer, and Social Activist* (Frankfort am Main: Peter Lang, 2009). (b) Margaret Hope Bacon, *Let This Life Speak: The Legacy of Henry Joel Cadbury* (Philadelphia: University of Pennsylvania Press, 1987). See Margaret Hope Bacon, *Henry J. Cadbury: Scholar, Activist, Disciple,* pamphlet #376 (Wallingford, PA: Pendle Hill, 2005), and Os Cresson, "Henry Joel Cadbury: No Assurance of God or Immortality," in David Boulton, ed., *Godless for God's Sake: Nontheism in Contemporary Quakerism* (Dent, Cumbria, UK: Dales Historical Monographs, 2006), 85–90.

52. George Santayana, *Little Essays Drawn from the Writings of George Santayana*, ed. Logan Pearsall Smith (NY: Charles Scribner, 1920). Reprinted in 1921, '24 and '31.

53. Rufus Jones, *Some Exponents of Mystical Religion* (New York: Abingdon Press, 1930), 9–12.

54. Rufus Jones, *Pathways to the reality of God* (New York: Macmillan, 1931), 155; *The Trail of Life in the Middle Years* (New York: Macmillan, 1934), 166; *Testimony of the Soul* (New York: Macmillan, 1936), 36; *Some Problems of Life*, (Nashville: Cokesbury Press, 1937), 76; *New Eyes for Invisibles* (New York: Macmillan, 1943), 80; and *A Call to What is Vital* (New York: Macmillan, 1948), 18.

55. Henry J. Cadbury, "My Personal Religion," 22–31.

56. Henry J. Cadbury, *The Character of A Quaker,* pamphlet #103 (Wallingford, PA: Pendle Hill, 1959). Also in "Two Strands in Quakerism," *Friends Journal* 5, no. 14 (April 4, 1959): 212–14.

Quaker Outreach to Scientists

57. http://www.quakerearthcare.org.

58. Elton Trueblood, "Present Secular Philosophies," in John Kavanaugh, *The Quaker Approach to Contemporary Problems* (NY: G. P. Putnam's Sons, 1953).

59. Jocelyn Bell Burnell, in *Beautiful Minds,* television documentary, dir. Jacqui Farnham (BBC Four, April 12, 2010), http://www.bbc.co.uk.

60. James H. Leuba, *The Belief in God and Immortality: A Psychological, Anthropological, and Statistical Study* (Boston: Sherman, French, 1916), and James H. Leuba, "Religious Beliefs of American Scientists" *Harper's Magazine* 169 (1934):291–300. (b) Edward J. Larson and Larry Witham, "Leading Scientists Still Reject God" *Nature* 394, no. 6691 (1998): 313.

61. Kenneth Boulding, "Machines, Men, and Religion," *Friends Journal* 14, no. 24 (December 15, 1968): 643–44.

62. T. Noel Stern, "Jesse Holmes, Liberal Quaker," *Friends Journal* 38, no. 6 (1992): 21–23. See Albert J. Wahl, *Jesse Herman Holmes, 1864–1942: A Quaker's Affirmation for Man* (Richmond IN: Friends United Press, 1979).

63. "Quaker Revival," *Time Magazine*, December 10, 1928, 43–44.

64. Jesse Holmes, "To the Scientifically-Minded," *Friends Intelligencer* 85, no. 6 (1928): 103–04. Reprinted in *Friends Journal* 38, no. 6 (June 1992): 22–23. Also published as *To the Scientifically-Minded* (Philadelphia: Friends General Conference, undated), and *A Los Intelectuales* (Philadelphia: Friends General Conference, undated).

65. Jesse Holmes, "The Quakers and the Sciences," *Friends Intelligencer* 88, no. 6 (1931): 537–38.

66. (a) http://www.quakerearthcare.org. (b) Spiritual Nurturance Committee of Quaker Earthcare Witness, "Statement on Unity with

Diversity" *BeFriending Creation* 26, no. 3 (May-June 2013): 9, http://www.quakerearthcare.org.

Roots and Flowers of Quaker Nontheism

Part I: Roots of Quaker Nontheism

67. Gerrard Winstanley, *The Law of Freedom in a Platform, or True Magistracey Restored* (1652), in Gerrard Winstanley, *The Works of Gerrard Winstanley,* ed. George H. Sabine (Ithaca, New York: Russell & Russell, 1965), 501–600.

68. Gerrard Winstanley, *The Law of Freedom,* 104–05.

69. Gerrard Winstanley, *The New Law of Righteousness*, in Gerrard Winstanley, *The Works of Gerrard Winstanley,* 170.

70. Jacob Bauthumley, *The Light and Dark Sides of God, Or a plain and brief Discourse of the Light side (God, Heaven and Earth) The dark side (Devill, Sin, and Hell)* (London: William Learner, 1650).

71. (a) David Scofield Wilson, *In the Presence of Nature* (Amherst MA: University of Massachusetts Press, 1978), 92. (b) John Bartram to Peter Collinson, June 11, 1743, William Darlington and Peter Collinson, eds., *Memorials of John Bartram and Humphrey Marshall* (New York: Hafner, 1967), 164. (c) John Bartram to Benjamin Rush, December 5, 1767, Thomas P. Slaughter, *The Natures of John and William Bartram* (Philadelphia: University of Pennsylvania Press, 2005) 62.

72. William Darlington and Peter Collinson, eds., *Memorials of John Bartram,* 398.

73. Charles Wetherill, *History of the Free Quakers* (Washington. D.C.: Ross & Perry, 2002), 48.

74. Charles Wetherill, *Free Quakers,* 32.

75. Hannah Barnard, in Thomas Foster, *An Appeal to the Society of Friends on the Primitive Simplicity of their Christian Principles and Church Discipline; and on Some Recent Proceedings in the Said Society* (London: J. Johnson, 1801), 122–23.

76. Hannah Barnard to William Matthews, September 6, 1802, William Matthews, *The Recorder* (London: J. Johnson, 1802).

165

77. Elias Hicks, in Bliss Forbush, *Elias Hicks: Quaker Liberal* (NY: Columbia University Press, 1956), 78.

78. Elias Hicks, in Norma Jacob, *Introducing . . . Elias Hicks: A Condensation of Bliss Forbush's Original Biography* (Philadelphia: Friends General Conference, 1984), 19.

79. David Duncan, *'Essays and Reviews.' A Lecture* (Manchester, UK: Edwin Slater, 1861), 8.

80. Friends at the Memorial Hall, Manchester, "Address Adopted by the Friends at the Memorial Hall, Manchester," *The Manchester Friend* 2, no. 12 (1873), 190.

81. Joseph B. Forster, *On Liberty. An Address to the Members of the Society of Friends* (London: F. Bowyer Kitto and Sutherland: W. H. Hills, 1867), 26.

82. Joseph B. Forster, editorial, *The Manchester Friend* 1, no. 1 (1871), 1, italics in the original.

83. Joseph B. Forster, editorial, 1871, 2.

84. Joseph B. Forster, editorial, *The Manchester Friend* 2, no. 12 (1873), 189, italics in the original.

85. George S. Brady, "State of the Society of Friends" *The Manchester Friend* 2, no. 10 (1873), 168.

86. Elizabeth Isichei, *Victorian Quakers* (Oxford: Oxford University Press, 1970), 30–32.

87. Christopher Densmore, "Be Ye Therefore Perfect: Anti-Slavery and the Origins of the Yearly Meeting of Progressive Friends in Chester County, Pennsylvania," *Quaker History* 93, no. 2 (2004), 28–46.

88. Oliver Johnson, Message during yearly meeting in Waterloo NY, June 3, 1855, in the *Proceedings of the Annual Meeting of Friends of Human Progress* (Syracuse NY: Evening Chronicle Print, 1855), 5.

89. (a) Christopher Densmore, "Be Ye Therefore Perfect," 41. (b) Pennsylvania Yearly Meeting of Friends, *Exposition of Sentiments* (1853), http://www.quest.quaker.org.

90. (a) Lucretia Mott to Mary P. Allen, June 5, 1877, in Anna Davis Hallowell, ed., *James and Lucretia Mott: Life and Letters* (Boston: Houghton Mifflin, 1890), 460. (b) Lucretia Mott, "When the Heart Is

Attuned to Prayer," in Dana Greene, ed. , *Lucretia Mott: Her Complete Speeches and Sermons* (NY: Edwin Mellen, 1980), 302. (c) Lucretia Mott to James L. Pierce, January 15, 1849, in Anna Davis Hallowell, *James and Lucretia Mott,* 315.

91. Lucretia Mott, in Edward T. James, Janet Wilson James and Paul S. Boyer, *Notable American Women 1607–1950: A Biographical Dictionary,* vol. 2 (Cambridge, MA: Belknap Press of Harvard University Press, 1975), 592–95.

92. Lucretia Mott, address at annual meeting of the Free Religious Association, June 2, 1871, in Anna Davis Hallowell, *James and Lucretia Mott,* 551.

93. Lucretia Mott, conversation with Elizabeth Cady Stanton, 1840, in Anna Davis Hallowell, *James and Lucretia Mott,* 188.

94. Maria Mitchell, *Maria Mitchell: Life, Letters and Journals,* ed. Phebe Mitchell Kendall (Boston: Lee and Shepard, 1896), (a) 241; (b) 241; (c) 176.

95. Maria Mitchell, *Life, Letters and Journals,* 243–44.

96. (a) Susan B. Anthony, "Divine Discontent," in Lynn Sherr, *Failure is Impossible: Susan B. Anthony In Her Own Words* (NY: Random House, 1995), notes 17, 20, 6, and 32. (b) Susan B. Anthony, address to Pennsylvania Yearly Meeting of Progressive Friends at Longwood, PA, 1873, in *Proceedings of the Pennsylvania Yearly Meeting of Progressive Friends Held at Longwood, Chester County* (NY: Baker & Godwin, 1873) 56.

97. Elizabeth Cady Stanton, *Eighty Years and More: Reminiscences, 1815–1897* (Boston: Northeastern University Press, 1993), 44.

98. Elizabeth Cady Stanton, "The Pleasures of Age," speech on November 12, 1885, *The Selected Papers of Elizabeth Cady Stanton and Susan B. Anthony,* vol. 4, ed. Ann D. Gordon (New Brunswick, NJ: Rutgers University Press, 2006), 459.

99. (a) Elizabeth Cady Stanton, Harriot Stanton and Blatch Stanton, *Elizabeth Cady Stanton as Revealed in her Letters, Diary and Reminiscences* (NY: Harper & Brothers, 1922), 239. (b) Elizabeth Cady Stanton, *Bible and Church Degrade Women* (Chicago: H. L. Green, [1898]), 6.

100. Joseph Rowntree, *Memorandum on the Declaration of Christian*

Doctrine issued by the Richmond Conference, 1887 (York, UK, 5th month 10, 1888).

101. William Littleboy, *The Appeal of Quakerism to the Non-Mystic* (Harrowgate, UK: Committee of Yorkshire Quarterly Meeting of the Society of Friends, 1916). Reprinted by the Friends Literature Committee, Yorkshire, 1938, and by Friends Book Centre, London, 1945.

102. Henry J. Cadbury, *Quakerism and Early Christianity* (London: Allen & Unwin, 1957).

103. Arthur S. Eddington, *Science and the Unseen World* (NY: Macmillan, 1929), 87–89.

104. (a) John Linton. "Quakerism as Forerunner," *Friends Journal* 25, no. 17 (October 15, 1979): 4–9. Reprinted as *Quakerism as Forerunner*, pamphlet #1 (London: Quaker Universalist Group, 1979). Also in Quaker Universalist Fellowship. *The Quaker Universalist Reader Number 1: A Collection of Essays, Addresses and Lectures* (Landenberg, PA: printed by author, 1991), 1. (b) Daniel A. Seeger, "Is Coexistence Possible?," *Friends Journal* 30, no. 12 (1984): 11–14. Also in *Quaker Universalist Reader Number 1* (Laudenberg, PA: Quaker Universalist Fellowship, 1986), 85.

Part II: Flowers of Quaker Nontheism

105. Jesse Holmes, "To the Scientifically-Minded," *Friends Intelligencer* 85, no. 6 (1928): 103–04. Reprinted in *Friends Journal* 38, no. 6 (June 1992): 22–23. Also published as *To the Scientifically-Minded* (Philadelphia: Friends General Conference, undated), and *A Los Intelectuales* (Philadelphia: Friends General Conference, undated).

106. (a) Jesse Holmes, *The Modern Message of Quakerism*, Philadelphia: Friends General Conference, 1912. Also published as *What is Truth?* Philadelphia: Friends General Conference (undated). (b) Jesse Holmes, "The Quakers and the Sciences," *Friends Intelligencer* 88, no. 6 (1931): 537–38.

107. Jesse Holmes, "'Our Christianity'?" *Universalist Friends* 39 (Fall & Winter, 2003): 15–22.

108. Henry J. Cadbury, "My Personal Religion," *Universalist Friends*

35 (Fall-Winter 2000): 22–31, with corrections in 36 (Spring-Summer 2000): 18. Also see Henry J. Cadbury, "My Personal Religious Beliefs," brief notes for a talk at Harvard Divinity School (unpublished manuscript, 1940). For another interpretation of Cadbury's writings, see Paul Anderson, "Is 'Nontheist Quakerism' a Contradiction of Terms?" *Quaker Religious Thought* 118 (May 2012): 5–24.

109. Henry J. Cadbury, *Quakerism and Early Christianity,* (London: Allen & Unwin, 1957), 47–48.

110. Arthur Morgan, "Universal Brotherhood in Religion," *Friends Intelligencer* (October 17, 1953): 558 and 564.

111. Arthur Morgan, letter, *The New Humanist,* 6 (May-June, 1933).

112. Arthur Morgan, "Necessity," talk at Yellow Springs Monthly Meeting, June 20, 1968, in Walter Kahoe, *Arthur Morgan: A Biography and Memoir* (Moylan, PA: The Whimsie Press, 1977).

113. Morris Mitchell, *World Education—Revolutionary Concept* (NY: Pageant Press, 1967).

114. Bart Sobel. "Morris Mitchell: Prophet of World Education" (PhD dissertation, Boston University, 1971.), University Microfilms, Ann Arbor, MI.

115. "Burtt Explains Quaker Faith," *The Cornell Daily Sun*, April 4, 1951, p. 3, http://cdsun.library.cornell.edu.

116. Richard S. Peters, *Reason, Morality and Religion*, Swarthmore Lecture (London: Friends Home Service Committee, 1972). Also in Richard S. Peters, *Reason and Compassion* (London and Boston: Routledge & K. Paul, 1973).

117. Staughton Lynd, "The Whole Kit and Caboodle," *The KIT Newsletter* 7, no. 1 (1995), http://www.perefound.org.

118. Alice Lynd and Staughton Lynd, *Liberation Theology for Quakers*, pamphlet #326 (Walingford, PA: Pendle Hill, 1996). Reprinted in Staughton Lynd, *Living Inside our Hope: A Steadfast Radical's Thoughts on Rebuilding the Movement* (Ithaca, NY: Cornell University Press, 1997), 44.

119. Alice Lynd and Staughton Lynd, *Liberation Theology,* 62–63, italics in the original.

120. (a) Claire Walker, "Must We Feel Comfortable?" *Friends Journal*

9, no. 15 (August 1, 1963): 334. (b) Joseph Havens, "Christian Roots and Post-Christian Horizons" *Friends Journal* 10, no. 1 (January 1, 1964): 5–8. (c) Lawrence McK. Miller, Jr., "The 'Honest to God' Debate and Friends" *Friends Journal* 10, no. 6 (March 15, 1964): 124–26. (d) Letters by Howard Kershner, Albert Schreiner and Mary Louise O'Hara in *Friends Journal*, April 1, May 15 and July 15, 1964. (e) For more on this, see: Os Cresson, "Reviews of Publications on Quaker Nontheism in the 1960s" (unpublished manuscript), http://nontheistfriends.org.

121. Workshop for Non-Theistic Friends, "Seekers Beyond Tradition" *Friends Journal* 22, no. 19 (November 15, 1976): 586–87. Slightly edited version of unpublished report by participants in the Workshop for Non-Theistic Friends held at the Friends General Conference Gathering, Ithaca NY, June 26–July 3, 1976, http://www.nontheistfriends.org. Workshop also described in Robert Morgan, "Some Surprises For Us?" *Friends Journal* 22, no. 19 (November 15, 1976): 582–83.

122. John Linton, letter, "A Universalist Group," *The Friend* 136 (April 21, 1978): 484. See John Linton, letter, "A Universalist Group" *The Friend* 136 (October 20, 1978): 1315.

123. John Linton, "Quakerism as Forerunner." *Friends Journal* 25, no. 17 (October 15, 1979): 4–9. Reprinted as *Quakerism as Forerunner,* pamphlet #1 (London: Quaker Universalist Group, 1979). Also in Quaker Universalist Fellowship, *The Quaker Universalist Reader Number 1: A Collection of Essays, Addresses and Lectures* (Landenberg, PA: printed by author, 1986), 1–13.

124. Kingdon W. Swayne, "Confessions of a Post-Christian Agnostic," *Friends Journal* 26, no. 3 (February 15, 1980): 6–9. Also in Quaker Universalist Fellowship. *Variations on the Quaker Message* (Landenberg, PA: printed by author, 1990), 1–6.

125. Kingdon W. Swayne, "Universalism or Latitudinarianism?," *Universalist Friends* 7 (1986): 8–11.

126. Kingdon W. Swayne, "Universalism and Me—3 Friends Respond," *Universalist Friends* 23 (1994): 9–10.

127. Eric Johnson, "Why I Am an Atheist." *Friends Journal* 37, no. 1

(January 1991): 17. Reprinted in Quaker Universalist Fellowship, *Variations on the Quaker Message,* pamphlet #201 (Landenberg, PA: printed by author, 1991).

128. Eric Johnson, "Atheism and Friends," letter, *Friends Journal* 37, no. 5 (May 1991): 6.

129. (a) David Rush, "Facts and Figures: Do Quakers Believe in God, and if They Do, What Sort of God?," in David Boulton, ed., *Godless for God's Sake: Nontheism in Contemporary Quakerism* (Dent, Cumbria, UK: Dales Historical Monographs, 2006), 91–100. Also see Mark S. Cary and Anita L. Weber, "Two Kinds of Quakers: A Latent Class Analysis," *Quaker Studies* 12/1 (2007): 134–144. (b) David Rush, "They Too Are Quakers: A Survey of 199 Nontheist Friends," *The Woodbrooke Journal* 11 (Winter 2002). Reprinted as *They Too Are Quakers: A Survey of 199 Nontheist Friends* (Millsboro, VA: Quaker Universalist Fellowship, 2003).

130. (a) Robin Alpern, "Reflections on a Decade of Nontheism Workshops" (unpublished manuscript, 2007), http://www.nontheistfriends .org. (b) David Boulton, "Nontheism Among Friends: Its History and Theology" (paper delivered at the Quaker Theological Discussion Group meeting at the American Society for Biblical Literature Conference, San Francisco CA, November 2011).

131. http://www.nontheistfriends.org.

132. Nontheist Friends Network, report, April 27, 2011, http://www. nontheistfriends.org.

133. (a) David Boulton, ed., "New Nontheist Friends Network in Britain", last modified April 27, 2011, http://www.nontheistfriends.org. (b) quoted in David Boulton, "Nontheism Among Friends."

134. David Boulton, ed., *Godless for God's Sake.*

135. Chuck Fager, review, "Godless for God's Sake: Nontheism in Contemporary Quakerism," *Quaker Theology* 13 (2007), http://www.quest. quaker.org.

136. Henry Cadbury (?), "The Separation in the Society of Friends, 1827." *Friends Intelligencer* 71, no. 9 (Second month 28, 1914): 129–132. Also published as Henry Cadbury (?), *Differences in Quaker Belief In 1827 and To-Day* (Philadelphia: Biddle Press, 1914).

137. Margaret Hope Bacon, *Let This Life Speak: The Legacy of Henry Joel Cadbury* (Philadelphia: University of Pennsylvania Press, 1987), 26.

138. Spiritual Nurturance Committee of Quaker Earthcare Witness, "Statement on Unity with Diversity," *BeFriending Creation* 26, no. 3 (May-June 2013): 9, http://www.quakerearthcare.org.

Religious Naturalism in the Time of Fox

139. Rufus M. Jones, *Mysticism and Democracy in the English Commonwealth* (NY: Octagon Books, 1965). See Rufus M. Jones, *Studies in Mystical Religion* (London: Macmillan, 1909), and Rufus M. Jones, *Spiritual Reformers in the 16th and 17th Century* (Gloucester MA: Peter Smith, 1971).

140. Christopher Hill, *The World Turned Upside Down: Radical Ideas During the English Revolution* (NY: Viking Press, 1972), 165.

141. Daniel A. Seeger, "Why Do the Unbelievers Rage? The New Atheists and the Universality of the Light," *Friends Journal* 56, no. 1 (January 2010): 6–11.

142. George Fox, *The Journal of George Fox*, revised edition, ed. John L. Nickalls (Philadelphia: Religious Society of Friends, 1985), 25.

"Creation is God himself"

143. (a) Jacob Bauthumley, *The Light and Dark Sides of God, Or a plain and brief Discourse of the Light side (God, Heaven and Earth) The dark side (Devill, Sin, and Hell)* (London: William Learner, 1650). (b) George Fox, *The Journal,* 182, and Norman Cohn, *The Pursuit of the Millennium: Revolutionary Millenarians and Mystical Anarchists of the Middle Ages* (NY: Oxford University Press, 1970), 303, and John N. King, *Foxe's Book of Martyrs and Early Modern Print Culture* (New York: Cambridge University Press, 2006), 156.

144. (a) Gerrard Winstanley, *Fire in the Bush,* in Gerrard Winstanley, *The Works of Gerrard Winstanley,* 451. (b) Gerrard Winstanley, *The Law of Freedom in a Platform, or True Magistracey Restored,* in Gerrard

Winstanley, *The Works of Gerrard Winstanley,* 565. (c) Gerrard Winstanley, *The Law of Freedom,* 564.

145. David Boulton, *Gerrard Winstanley and the Republic of Heaven* (Dent, Cumbria, UK: Dales Historical Monographs, 1999). See David Boulton, *Militant Seedbeds of Early Quakerism* (Landenberg, PA: Quaker Universalist Fellowship, 2005), http://www.universalistfriends.org.

146. John Everard, *The Gospel Treasury Opened* (London: Rapha Harford, 1657), 19–20.

147. William Penn, in Rufus M. Jones, *Mysticism and Democracy,* 77–78.

148. Rufus M. Jones, *Mysticism and Democracy,* 77–78.

149. (a) Richard Coppin, *A Hint of the Glorious Mystery of Divine Teachings* (1649), 8, in Christopher Hill, *The World Turned Upside Down,* 220–21. (b) William Penn to John Rodes, 1693, in Allen C. Thomas, "William Penn on the Choice of Books," *Bulletin of the Friends Historical Society* 4 (1911), 36.

150. (a) Thomas Edwards, *Gangrena,* vol. 1 (London: Ralph Smith, 1646), 21. (b) Edward Hyde, *A Wonder and yet no Wonder: A Great Red Dragon in Heaven* (London: Giles Calvert, 1650), 24.

151. (a) Jacob Boehme, *Aurora: The Day-Spring, or, Dawning of the Day in the East; or, Morning-Redness in the Rising of the Sun: That is, The Root or Mother of Philosophy, Astrology, and Theology, from the True Ground: Or, A Description of Nature . . . All set down from a true Ground in the Knowledge of the Spirit, and by the Impulse of God,* eds. Charles James Barker and D. S. Hehner (Edmonds, WA: Sure Fire Press, 1992), italics in the original. (b) Jacob Boehme, *The Confessions of Jacob Boehme and the Way to Christ,* ed. W. Scott Palmer (Whitefish, MT: Kessinger Publishing, 1992), 56. (c) Jacob Boehme, *Theoscopia or The highly Precious Gate of the Divine Intuition showing what* Mysterium Magnum *is, and how all is from, through and in God; how God is so near all things, and fills all* (Sequim, WA: Holmes Publishing, 1989), chapter 3, para. 13.

152. Rufus M. Jones, *Mysticism and Democracy,* 134–35 and 220, and Rufus M. Jones, *Spiritual Reformers,* 170, note 6. See Andrew Weeks,

Boehme: An Intellectual Biography of the Seventeenth-Century Philosopher and Mystic (Albany, NY: State University of New York Press, 1991), 221–22.

153. (a) Baruch Spinoza to Henry Oldenburg, 1662, in Lewis S. Feuer, *Spinoza and the Rise of Liberalism* (New Brunswick, NJ: Transaction, 1987), 54–55. (b) Baruch Spinoza, *Ethics*, trans. Edwin Curley (Princeton, NJ: Princeton University Press, 1985), Part IV, Preface. (c) Richard H. Popkin and Michael A. Signer *Spinoza's Earliest Publication? The Hebrew Translation of Margaret Fell's* A Loving Salutation (Wolfeboro, NH: Van Gorcum, 1987), 7. See Henry J. Cadbury, "Spinoza and a Quaker Document of 1657," *Mediaeval and Renaissance Studies*, vol. 1 (London: Warbur Institute, 1941), 130–32. (d) Peter Balling, *Light upon the Candlestick,* eds. Rufus Jones, Sally Rickerman and Kingdon Swayne (Landenberg, PA: Quaker Universalist Fellowship, 1992), 129, 12–13, and 131–32. (e) Henry W. Robinson and Walter Adams, eds., *The Diary of ROBERT HOOKE, M.A. M.D. F.R.S., 1672–1680* (London: Taylor & Francis, 1935), 368.

154. (a) John Toland, *Socinianism Truly Stated . . . by a pantheist* (London, 1705). (b) John Toland, *Pantheisticon* (NY: Garland Publishing, 1976), 70. (c) John Toland, *Pantheisticon,* 15.

155. British History Online, http://www.britishhistory.ac.uk.

156. George Fox, *The Journal*, 295–96, 303, and 318.

157. George Fox, *The Journal*, 274.

"All things come by nature"

158. George Fox. *The Journal,* 25.

159. (a) William Sewel, *The History of the Rise, Increase and Progress of the Christian People called Quakers . . .* (London: J. Sowle, 1722) 16–17. See The Yearly Meeting of the Religious Society of Friends (Quakers) in Britain, *Quaker Faith and Practice* (London: printed by author, 1995), #26.02. (b) John Greenleaf Whittier, *The Writings of John Greenleaf Whittier,* vol. II (London: Macmillan, 1888), 342–44, http://www.kimopress.com.

160. William C. Braithwaite, *The Beginnings of Quakerism* (London: Macmillan, 1923), 38, note 1.

161. (a) Lodowicke Muggleton, *The Acts of the Witnesses*, ed. Ted L. Underwood (NY: Oxford University Press, 1999), 18–20 and 38–40, italics in the original. (b) Lodowicke Muggleton, *A True Interpretation of the Eleventh Chapter of the 11th Revelation of St. John*, in *The Works of John Reeve and Lodowicke Muggleton,* vol. 3 (London: E. Brown, 1833), 49.

162. Jacob Boehme, *The Confessions of Jakob Boehme*, 46.

163. Timothy Stubbs, *The Ranters Declaration,* in James C. Davis, *Fear, Myth and History: The Ranters and the Historians* (Cambridge: Cambridge University Press, 1986), 176.

164. Alexander Agnew, known as Jock of Broad Scotland (1651), in David Masson, *The Life of John Milton* (Gloucester Massachusetts: Peter Smith, 1965), 93–94, and Christopher Hill, *The World Turned Upside Down,* 167–68. Also, John Rogers (1578) and John Strype (1709) in Ernest Belfort Bax, *Rise and Fall of the Anabaptists* (NY: Macmillan, 1903), 356 and 365.

165. Lucy Apsley Hutchinson, *Memoirs of the Life of Colonel Hutchinson, Governor of Nottingham*, ed. N. H. Keeble (London: Phoenix, 2000), 105–06.

166. (a) George Fox, *The Journal,* 42, note. (b) Lucy Apsley Hutchinson, *Life of Colonel Hutchinson,* 105–06; and William Howie Wylie, *Old and New Nottingham* (London: Longman, Brown, Green, and Longmans, 1853), 156.

167. Jacob Boehme, *The Confessions of Jacob Boehme,* 165–66, 175–76.

168. Thomas Aquinas, *Summa Theologica*, vol. 1, part 1 (NY: Cosimo, 2007), 13–14.

169. Hermes Trismegistus, *The Pymander of Hermes,* ed. William Wynn Westcott, trans. John Everard (London: Theosophical Publishing Society, 1894), 21–23. http://www.rexresearch.com/alchemy5/poemander.htm#b2.

170. (a) Marcus Aurelius, *Meditations* (Baltimore: Penguin Books,

1964), 4th Book, IV, #23. (b) Marcus Aurelius, trans. Meric Casaubon, *The Golden Book of Marcus Aurelius* (London: Meric Casaubon, 1634). (c) William Penn to John Rodes, 1693, in Allen C. Thomas, "William Penn on the Choice of Books," *Bulletin of the Friends Historical Society* 4 (1911), 33–42.

171. Titus Lucretius Carus, *On the Nature of Things / Lucretius,* trans. by William Ellery Leonard (Mineola NY: Dover, 2004), Book 1, line 160–164. See Stephen Greenblatt, *The Swerve: How the World Became Modern* (NY: W. W. Norton, 2011).

172. (a) Titus Lucretius Carus, trans. Lucy Hutchinson, *Lucy Hutchinson's Translation of Lucretius, De Rerum Natura* (London: Gerald Duckworth, and Ann Arbor, MI: University of Michigan Press, 1996). (b) Lucy Apsley Hutchinson, *Life of Colonel Hutchinson,* Appendix.

173. John Evelyn, *An Essay on the First Book of T. Lucretius Carus De Rerum Natura* (London: G. Bedle and T. Collins, 1656), and Thomas Creech, *T. Lucretius Carus the Epicurean Philosopher* (Oxford: Anthony Stephens, 1682).

"Unity with the creation"

174. George Fox, *The Journal,* 27.

175. George Fox, *The Journal,* 19, 28, 29, and 33.

176. George Fox, *The Journal,* 2

177. George Fox, *The Journal,* 110. See Geoffrey F. Nuttall, "'Unity with the Creation': George Fox and the Hermetic Philosophy," *Friend's Quarterly* 1 (January, 1947): 134–143.

178. Marcus Aurelius, *Meditations,* 4th Book, XXXVI, 38.

179. William Penn, *Some Fruits of Solitude, in Reflections and Maxims* (NY: Scott-Thaw, 1903), xxv.

180. David Duncan, *John Woolman: A Paper at the Friends Institute, Manchester* (London: F. Bowyer Kitto and Manchester: W. Hale, 1871), 34–35.

"We show you the Deity"

181. Job 12:7–10; Psalm 19:1–4; Romans 1:20.

182. Jacob Boehme, *The Signature of All Things and Other Writings* (Cambridge, UK: James Clark, 1969), 17.

183. Gerrard Winstanley, *The Law of Freedom,* 580.

184. William Penn, *Some Fruits of Solitude,* 4, italics in the original.

185. Michael Hunter, *Robert Boyle, 1627–91: Scrupulosity and Science* (Rochester, NY: Boydell Press, 2000), 29.

186. John Bartram to Peter Collinson, Dec. 3, 1762, in John Bartram to Peter Collinson, June 11, 1743, in William Darlington and Peter Collinson, eds., *Memorials of John Bartram and Humphrey Marshall* (New York: Hafner, 1967), 243.

"An ocean of light and love"

187. Jacob Boehme, *Aurora,* 66–70.

188. (a) George Fox, *The Journal,* 11. (b) Gerrard Winstanley, *The Mysterie of God, Concerning the Whole Creation, Mankinde,* in Gerrard Winstanley, *The Works of Gerrard Winstanley,* 82. (c) Joseph Salmon, *Heights in Depths and Depths in Heights, or Truth no less Secretly than Sweetly Sparkling out of its Glory from under a Cloud of Obloquie* (London: Tho. Newcomb, 1651). See Douglas Gwyn, "Joseph Salmon from Seeker to Ranter—and Almost to Quaker," *Journal of the Friends Historical Society* 58, no. 2 (1998), 114–31. (d) http://www.sofn.org.uk.

189. John Everard, *The Gospel Treasury Opened,* 753.

190. (a) John Everard, *The Gospel Treasury Opened,* 425. (b) John Milton, *Paradise Regained* (London: John Starkey, 1671), 94–95. (c) Isaac Newton, in Isaac Newton, *Principia,* ed. Stephen Hawking (Philadelphia: Running Press, 2002), xviii.

"Likeness to Christ rather than notions of Christ"

191. (a) Rapha Harford, "The Epistle Dedicatory," in John Everard, *The Gospel Treasury Opened,* [n.p.]. (b) William Penn, *An Address to Protestants of all Persuasions,* in William Penn, *The Select Works of William Penn, vol. 3, 4th ed.* (London: William Phillips, 1825), 83. (c) Lu-

cretia Mott, "Likeness to Christ" (1849), in Lucretia Mott, *Lucretia Mott: Her Complete Speeches and Sermons*, Dana Greene, ed. (NY: Edwin Mellen, 1980), 107. See Margaret Hope Bacon, *Valiant Friend: The Life of Lucretia Mott* (Philadelphia: Friends General Conference, 1999), 43.

192. Letter from the Meeting of Elders at Balby, 1656, in Philadelphia Yearly Meeting. *Faith and Practice* (Philadelphia: printed by author, 2001), Foreword.

193. John Everard, *The Gospel Treasury Opened,* 292.

194. (a) Christopher Hill, *The World Turned Upside Down,* 115. (b) Hendrick Niclaes, *An Introduction to the Holy Understanding of the Glass of Righteousnesse* (London: George Whittington, 1649), 87.

195. Gerrard Winstanley, *An Appeale to all Englishmen,* in Gerrard Winstanley, *The Works of Gerrard Winstanley,* 408–09.

196. John Everard, *The Gospel Treasury Opened,* 344.

197. (a) Norman Cohn, *The Pursuit of the Millennium,* 31. (b) Augustine of Hippo, Homilies on the First Epistle of John, in *Nicene and Post-Nicene Fathers: First Series, vol. 7,* ed. Philip Schaff (NY: Cosimo, 2007), 504.

198. (a) Henry Cadbury, "Quaker Principles and Action," notes for talk at Stony Brook, MD, 1962, 1–2, in Henry J. Cadbury Papers, Quaker Collection, Haverford College, Haverford, PA. (b) Henry Cadbury, *The Character of A Quaker,* pamphlet #103 (Wallingford, PA: Pendle Hill, 1959), 20. Also in "Two Strands in Quakerism," *Friends Journal* 5, no. 14 (April 4, 1959): 212–14.

199. (a) Samuel M. Janney, *The Life of William Penn; With Selections from His Correspondence and Auto-Biography,* 2nd ed. (Philadelphia: Lippincott, Grambo, 1852), 51. Also see "Traditional History," *Friends Intelligencer* 12, no. 8 (May 12, 1855): 120–21. (b) For another interpretation, see G. F. of Mahnacock, Long Island (perhaps Gideon Frost of Matinecock), "Traditional History," *Friends Intelligencer* 12, no. 8 (May 12, 1855): 116; and J. William Frost, "'Wear the Sword as Long as Thou Canst'. William Penn in Myth and History," *Journal of the Friends Historical Society* 58, no. 2 (1998): 91–113.

"We cannot miss of being good Naturalists"

200. William Harvey, *Anatomical Exercises on the Generation of Animals* (London, 1651), in William Harvey, *The Works of William Harvey,* ed. Robert Willis (London: Sydenham Society, 1847), 211.

201. (a) Gerrard Winstanley, *The New Law of Righteousness*, in Gerrard Winstanley, *The Works of Gerrard Winstanley,* 227. (b) Gerrard Winstanley, *The Saints Paradice*, in Gerrard Winstanley, *The Works of Gerrard Winstanley,* 96. (c) Gerrard Winstanley, *The Law of Freedom,* 564–65.

202. Gerrard Winstanley, *The Law of Freedom,* 565.

203. (a) George Fox, *The Journal,* 345. (b) E. Jean Whittaker, *Thomas Lawson, 1630–1691: North Country Botanist, Quaker and Schoolmaster* (York, UK: Sessions Book Trust, 1986). (c) John H. Felts, "Richard Lower: Anatomist and Physiologist," *Annals of Internal Medicine* 132, no. 5 (2000): 420–23. (d) Anne Conway, *The Principles of the Most Ancient and Modern Philosophy,* eds. Allison P. Coudert and Taylor Corse (Cambridge UK: Cambridge University Press, 1996), 12, 41, 64, and 69. See Carol Stoneburner, Theodor Benfey, and Robert Kraus, eds., "Perspectives on the Seventeenth Century World of Viscountess Anne Conway," *Guilford Review* 23 (1986), 1–90. (e) Michael Hunter, *Robert Boyle.*

204. William Penn to John Aubrey, June 13, 1683, in *The Papers of William Penn,* vol. 2, eds. R. S. Dunn and M. M. Dunn (Philadelphia: University of Pennsylvania Press, 1981–87), 394–96.

205. William Penn, *Some Fruits of Solitude,* 2–4, italics in the original.

Made in the USA
San Bernardino, CA
20 November 2016